# BAAL SHEM TOV

### RABBI YISRAEL BEN ELIEZER
### THE LEGENDARY KABBALAH MASTER

# HEART OF PRAYER

## VOLUME III

## A TREATISE ON
## CHASSIDIC SUPPLICATION

By **Tzvi Meir Cohn**

BST Publishing
Cleveland, Ohio

First Printing 2010

Translation and Commentary by Rabbi Doctor Eliezer Shore
Editing, Organization, introductory material and layout by
Tzvi Meir Cohn

© 2002-2010 by Tzvi Meir Cohn
Cover Design by Aitan Levy
Printed in the United States of America

ISBN: 978-0-9792865-6-8
Library of Congress Control Number: 2010923225
Library of Congress subject heading:
1. Hasidim — Legends. 2. Baal Shem Tov, ca. 1698-1760 —
Legends. 3. Hasidism. 4. Mysticism Judaism. 5. Title. 6.
Hasidic Prayer


Manufactured in the United States of America
BST Publishing
Cleveland, OH 44124
info@bstpublishing.com
www.baalshemtov.com

# TABLE OF CONTENTS

# INTRODUCTION

The vast majority of the translations in this sefer were taken from the Sefer Baal Shem Tov, Parsha Noach. The source of each section was found in the Sefer Baal Shem Tov.

I would like to express my sincere gratitude to the many people who have made this book possible.

Rabbi Sholom Ber Chaikin for reading the manuscript of this book, checking for errors and catching various mistakes of fact and occasionally tone.

Rabbi Michoel Feinstein for editing the manuscript of this book.

Yehudit and Robert Schulman for editing the manuscript of this book.

My wife and muse, Basha. "Thank you, Basha."

May G•d, blessed be He, shower blessings on all those who have helped in the preparation of this book.

Of course, none of this would be possible without the Holy One, Blessed is He, whom I thank "exceedingly with my mouth; amid the many I will praise Him."

# PREFACE

Rabbenu Yisrael ben Eliezer, commonly known as the Baal Shem Tov (Master of the Good Name), adapted Kabbalistic ideas in his mystical approach to prayer. At the core of his approach is the belief that all is encompassed by G•d.

The Baal Shem Tov taught that the purpose of prayer is to penetrate physicality and have the experience of knowing the Divine vitality which infuses all things. To achieve this experience, as you will see in this sefer (book), requires the annihilation of the self through means such as con- templation that all is G•d. In this state, the ego is left behind and the soul soars to the upper worlds.

A foundation stone of the Baal Shem Tov's approach to living life according to the dictates of the Torah was the importance of prayer above other religious duties, even over the study of the Torah. Making prayer of paramount importance was an innovation of the Baal Shem Tov over the way followed by the majority of Jewish communities throughout Eastern Europe.

Prior to the Baal Shem Tov, it was the common belief that for a person to learn how to pray with great love and fear, it was necessary to give one's life over to the study of the Torah and the performance of Mitzvahs.

The Baal Shem Tov's attitude towards prayer can best be understood by his stress on the practice of deveikut, attachment to G•d. Briefly stated, the practice is that a person should always have G•d in their thoughts, seeing beneath appearances the Divine vitality which infuses all things. In other words, the only true reality is G•d. The material world, and, for that matter, the 'upper spiritual worlds' seem to be true reality. In fact, they are a kind of screen, which hides G•d from human eyes, but through which He can be seen if man's spiritual gaze is properly directed. With proper use of prayer, one can see the infinite, Divine power as it is manifesting the creation.

To achieve the state of deveikut as practiced by the Baal Shem Tov, one strives to attain the state of 'bittul ha-yesh," 'the annihilation of somethingness.' In this state, there is an awareness that G•d alone is true reality and that all finite things are dissolved in His unity. In the state of bittul ha-yesh, the soul can soar to G•d while the ego is left behind. This state is especially to be cultivated at the time of prayer. Thus, Hasidic prayer is essentially an exercise in forsaking the world and abandoning the lower self.

Another aspect of prayer stressed by the Baal Shem Tov was that prayer influenced the upper spiritual worlds. This principle was accepted without qualification by the Hasidic Rebbes that followed in the path of the Baal Shem Tov. Rabbi Jacob Joseph of Polonnoye, a very close disciple of the Baal Shem Tov, wrote "that this is why the prayers have to be recited verbally and it is not sufficient for a man to only think the prayers in his mind. Although G•d knows all thoughts, when a man gives verbal expression to his prayers he provides a 'vessel' through which Divine grace can flow into the material world. If the prayers are only thought, the Divine grace would only be capable of flowing into the spiritual 'vessels' provided by thought."

The Baal Shem Tov also explained to his followers that prayer is for the sake of G•d. More specifically, prayer is for the sake of the Shechinah (the Divine Presence; sometimes identified as the sephirah of Malkut or Knesset Israel [The collectivity of Jewish souls]). This concept is treated throughout classical Hasidic writings.

An example of the principle 'prayer is for the sake of G•d' is that a man should consider that whatever happens to him happens concurrently to the Shechinah. If the Hasid finds himself sick, for example, he should reflect that G•d wants him to be well again, and until he recovers from his illness, G•d's will is unfulfilled. His purpose, then, in praying for good health and a speedy recovery should be so that the Shechinah will no longer be unfulfilled.

This concept can be understood by how the Baal Shem Tov solved the contradiction between two passages in the Zohar. In one passage, it is said that whoever does not pray for his sustenance daily is of little faith. In another passage, scorn is poured on those who bark like dogs begging for food. According to the Baal Shem Tov there really is no contradiction. In one case, a man should not beg for his food solely for his own sake. The experience of lack of food is from the need of a man's vital soul for Divine vitality. Since this vitality is, in reality, that of the Shechinah, he should pray for the pain experienced by his vital soul, which is another way of saying that he should pray for the sake of the Shechinah.

G•d makes those who fear Him to have a de-sire, for prayer is called 'desire.' G•d puts this desire to pray for something into man's heart because the G•d-fearing man would have no desire to petition G•d for anything since 'there is no want to them that fear Him' [Psalm 34:10]. The G•d-fearing man says 'enough' to whatever G•d gives him. Consequently, G•d puts the thought of prayer into man's heart for He desires man's prayers. Therefore, the verse concludes: 'and He hears their cry and saves them' [Psalm 145:19].

Rebbe Reb Dov Ber (later known as the Mezritcher Maggid and the successor to the Baal Shem Tov) taught the following teaching: "Behold, when a man prays, G•d forbid that he should direct all his desire towards that corporeal thing for which he asks. Rather, he should have the following in mind. Our Rabbis teach that the cow wishes to feed the calf more than the calf wishes to be fed. This means that a giver has a greater desire to give than the beneficiary has the desire to receive. So it is with G•d. His delight in benefiting His creatures is greater than the delight felt by the people He benefits."

In other words, petitionary prayer should be to please G•d in His role as Giver. Knowing that G•d has this desire to give, the worshipper should ask, but never for his own sake. The paradox of petitionary prayer is that the man's request is real and that the satisfaction of the man's needs desired. But the true worshipper sees it all as the fulfillment of G•d's purpose. In the act of receiving, or requesting to receive, the righteous man becomes a giver because he assists G•d in attaining His desire to be a giver.

Since the righteous pray for the sake of the Shechinah, their prayers for particular things such as health, sustenance and family are not for the different satisfactions of fulfilling their own needs but are all for the lack in the Shechinah as evidenced by their own needs. The result is that all petitionary prayer, no matter how varied in relation to its particular requests, is basically one simple prayer, that the lack in the Shechinah be filled.

G•d searches each person's heart and knows all its secrets. Since it is the heart that He really wants, prayers that are recited with strong concentration and are inwardly sincere, are very pleasing to Him and therefore these prayers are answered.

The holy Baal Shem Tov emphasized that G•d paid special attention to the spiritual service of an ordinary, but devout man. Those who follow(ed) the Baal Shem Tov's path with spiritual aspirations weren't satisfied with simple, thoughtless prayer.

Rather, they approached Hasidic prayer, as taught by Rabbenu Baal Shem Tov, as a rigorous, spiritual exercise with the goal of causing the self to be transcended so the soul can ascend to the spiritual worlds.

# CHAPTER 1

# PURPOSE
# OF PRAYER

1-1 Praying for the spiritual aspect of physical things.

**THE** requests in our prayers, such as those for livelihood or rain, are not for these physical things. Rather, they are directed at their supernal spiritual roots. Thus, in the physical is found only the external aspect of things; their spiritual aspects reside in the inner aspect of things.

Shemen Sasson, Psalms 86

∞

1-2 Praying in order to attach yourself Above.

**WHEN** you attach yourself Above during the Amidah[1], you will merit to be elevated on high during that prayer. As our Sages said, "A person who seeks to be purified will be helped."[2] Through this prayer, you can bind your thoughts to the Oneness Above. And then you will reach to an even greater level; that of being attached on High even when you are not engaged in prayer.

*Tzava'as HaRivash 37*

---

[1] Also referred to as the Shemonah Esreh (eighteen benedictions); the main section of daily prayer, recited standing and inaudibly.
[2] Talmud, *Shabbat* 104a

1-3 To cling to G•d, the Source of all desire.

**IT** is written, "A prayer of a poor man when he is faint [with an affliction] and pours out his tale of woe before G•d."[1]

The Baal Shem Tov explained this verse with the following parable.

In honor of his birthday, a king announced that he would distribute from his royal treasure house to whoever of his subjects was in need. Many people came with their requests, some asking for livelihood others for precious jewels. For each one of them, the king ordered his servants to fulfill their requests.

Now, there was one poor but wise man who was granted his one and only request, that he be given permission to speak with the king every day. As is known, there is nothing that the king's coffers lack because the king's wealth is so great; everything in the kingdom belongs to him. Thus, while the other people received their requests from the king's servants, who, by their very nature, are limited in that they are unable to give beyond that which the king had instructed; the wise man was able to ask the king, directly, on a daily basis for his needs and therefore was always able to obtain whatever he requested.

---

[1] Psalms 102:1

So too with a person who serves G•d by desiring to speak only to Him. All of G•d's goodness is given to him. This is why the "prayer for a poor man," asking only for the permission to speak with G•d everyday, "includes" all of his other prayers.

That is, when he pours out his woes before G•d and only requests to speak to the King Himself, then all of his prayers are answered by the Source of all desire.

*Me'or Einayim, Ki Seitzei*

∞

1-4 Prayer draws down Divine life-force.

**WORDS** of prayer create vessels to draw down shefah, the flow of Divine life-force into creation. Since G•d knows our thoughts, why do we have to pray? Because it is the words of prayer themselves that draw down the Divine life-force into the creation.

*Mevaser Tzedek, Terumah*

∞

1-5 Parable of how G•d puts us into different situations to arouse our awareness of His presence and our love for Him.

**THERE** was once a king who had a musician that could play the violin beautifully. The king loved one particular melody and requested that it be played in his chamber many times a day. Eventually, however, the melody became boring to the ears of the violinist; and he lost his previous enthusiasm and desire to play it.

What did the king do to fill him with fresh enthusiasm and drive? When he wanted to hear the melody, he brought in a random person from the street who had never heard it before. The new audience brought renewed energy and enthusiasm to the musician. Thus the king did for a long time.

Eventually, though, the king sought advice from his counselors about his musician, for it was getting difficult to always find a new person to bring in from the street. It was suggested that he permanently blind the musician, so that whenever the king wanted to hear his favorite melody, he would tell the musician that someone new had just come in the chamber, someone who had never heard it before. Since he could no longer see, he'd believe that someone new was really there. Then,

then the musician would be inspired with a fresh desire to play the melody so beloved by the king.

What does this parable mean? We pray to the King of Kings daily, pronouncing the same liturgy three times a day.[1] That is, every day we pray the exact same Amidah — morning, noon and night. Therefore, to us, our prayers become old or even boring. What does the King of the World do about this? Each day, He puts a person into different situations requiring His help. Then, G•d sends the person subtle hints and messages throughout the day that He is with him. Usually, He does this in the extraneous thoughts that come to the person. Of course, one must know how to interpret these thoughts. When the person believes that G•d is with him, he can summon the power to arouse in his heart a feeling of deep love and attachment to G•d.

When G•d grants a person insight and strong discernment, the person knows very well that no one prayer is ever like another, and whatever was spiritually lacking and subsequently repaired in the morning prayer could not have been so easily repaired in the afternoon and evening prayers. Everything depends on the [person's] or suppli-

---

[1] This refers to the Amidah, which is liturgically identical for each of the three weekday prayer services.

cant's clear perception in recognizing and properly interpreting everything he encounters in the world. Wherever he looks, he should be able to identify and therefore see Divinity enclothed there. And so long as he grasps the exaltation of G•d in new ways, and to be sure, in all ways, enthusiasm and longing are born in him to speak before G•d with fear and love, as though he has never prayed before. The King of Kings clearly perceives great yearning, love and innate caring to fully appreciate (within the scope of his ability) G•d's tangible and intangible presence in every aspect of his life experiences. The supplicant then becomes accustomed and even desirous to grasp His Majesty in the every facet of his life. Service to G•d, one of the three pillars of life[1] becomes a great delight to Him. G•d rejoices to call such a person wise and does not trouble Himself further to send him different hints. Rather, He takes away his vision of this lowly world and gives him a vision of the worlds that transcend time. Then, there is no division of the midot[2] at all, and everything is of equal value to him.

Once the person has achieved this level, where his vision of the worlds transcends time, his

---

[1] Pirkei Avos (Ethics of the Fathers) 1:2
[2] The Divine and mortal attributes of character, spiritual emotions and mental states.

service is always new. Further, since the person is then independent of time, he does not acquire the aspect of old age. Then, when he serves G•d with great desire and enthusiasm as well as with feelings of powerful love and attachment at every moment, it enables him to remain wholly and directly attached to Him. At this stage, it is good for him in this world and in the world to come. Amen!

*Ohr ha-Meir, Koheles, s.v. "Berabos Hatovah."*

∞

1-6 Causing prayers to ascend.

**THE** desires and intentions of an intelligent person that prays with his intellect do not physically ascend like pipe smoke leaving the mouth and ascending upwards. Rather, it is when a person's desire and intention are with feeling and enthusiasm that the prayers will ascend.

*Ohr HaMeir, Song of Songs*

∞

1-7 Praying for G•d's sake.

**PRAYERS** for physical needs, such as "Heal us and we shall be healed" and "Bless us with a good year,"[1] are like turning to a father who longs to fulfill his son's desires and to make sure that he lacks nothing, even so-called foolish things. For it is the nature of the One Who is Good to do good.

G•d's only thought is how to bestow material goodness on the Israelites, who are called His children. The words of prayer draw down sustenance and shefah into all the worlds, even into the material world so as to satisfy G•d's longing.

When you pray for yourself, Heaven scrutinizes your prayers to see if they are worthy of being received. But when you pray for the sake of G•d, nothing can stop your prayers from being received and accepted immediately.

*Kedushas Levi, Likutim Shonim p.509*

∞

1-8 Praying for a sick person.

**IF** a sick person prays for himself, the prayer can work because he repents for his own misdeeds.

---

[1] Prayers from the Amidah

But how do the prayers of others work on his behalf?

The answer is that prayer of others elevates the dinim,[1] located in the realm of Malchut (the realm of Divine Kingship), against the sick person to their root in the realm of Binah.[2] There, the dinim are sweetened and the letters creating the Divine judgments are recombined for good; for all Divine judgments are made with letter combinations.

*Rav Yeibi, Psalms 18*

∞

1-9 Effect of praying for another.

**IT** is written that when you pray on behalf of your friend for something that you need for yourself, your prayer will be answered first.[3] The reason is that when you pray for your friend, you uplift the Divine judgments against your friend, located in the realm of Gevurah,[4] to their source. Therefore, through the act of praying itself, you will

---

[1] Divine judgments
[2] Attribute of Understanding
[3] Talmud *Bava Kama* 92a
[4] Attribute of Severity

access the Supernal source of the Divine judgement in the realm of Gevurah, at which time your own needs will be addressed. Once there, you can also change the Divine judgment and cause healing to flow down on to the sick person.

*Me'or Einayim, Naso*

∞

1-10 Praying to reach new levels of understanding.

**THE** primary way to advance to new levels of understanding is to study Torah and pray with all of your strength. Then, you attach yourself to the Light of the Infinite, may He be blessed, that dwells within the letters of Torah and prayer. This infusion of Divine light subdues any physical inclination, and you can experience the abnegation or divestiture of your physical being. Then, you will enter the Supernal worlds and constantly rise to new levels of understanding and clarity.

*Toldos Aharon, Shelach*

∞

1-11 Praying well.

**IF** you can pray well, even once, you can up-lift all the lost prayers[1] that were previously left below. Together, all your prayers will be perfected and rise to the realm of Supernal Desire.

*Tiferes Shlomo, Shabbat Teshuva*

∞

1-12 Praying when suffering leads to revelation of G•d's kindness and deliverance.

**THE** light of the Shechinah is enwrapped in four types of suffering. Before all of the worlds were brought into actuality, these types of sufferings were hidden in G•d's essence. To G•d, the past, future and present are all one. The creation of the world meant that He transformed time from a potentiality into an actuality.

Before the Creation, there was no suffering, only glory, majesty, strength and joy. However, when G•d created all of the worlds, the ability to experience suffering and limitations[2] also came

---

[1] Those said without faith and cleaving to G•d
[2] Referring to constricted and narrow states of consciousness and existence; known as *mochin d'katnus*

about. Therefore, because of suffering and limitations, people pray with more effort. Through prayer, G•d's loving-kindness and deliverance to the world is revealed; for when you suffer and are in distress, you pray with greater spiritual attachment, concentration and intentions that are more pure.

*Ohr HaGanuz LaTzaddikim, Shemos*

∞

1-13 Praying for the sake of G•d.

**IT** is written, "In all their afflictions, He was afflicted"[1], and "I am with him in distress"[2]. This seems to be a contradiction with the statement in *Tikkunei Zohar*: "They cry out like dogs, but there is no one to wake in repentance to break out of their prison cell." Is G•d with us in our suffering or not?

The main repentance must be for His honor, which means rectifying and removing the agony caused by our sins. In all that you request, have in mind the honor of the Shechinah and pray that G•d's requests should be fulfilled. This is the meaning of, "May G•d fulfill all of your requests."[3]

---

[1] Isaiah 63:9
[2] Psalms 91:15
[3] Psalms 20:6

That is, all of your requests should be that G•d is fulfilled.[1] When your intentions are only for the sake of G•d, you cause the Divine Presence to ascend and create a Unification with Him.

*Mevaser Tzedek, Chukas*

∞

1-14 The ideal religious belief in G•d comes from both following the path of the forefathers and intellectual investigation.

**WHY** do we say "Our G•d and the G•d of our fathers?" Because there are two types of people who believe in G•d. The *first* believes in the Holy One because they follow the path of their forefathers, and remain strong in their faith. The second comes to religious belief through which investigation into the existence of G•d has been undertaken.

The first type of belief has the advantage of steadfastness that is impossible to entice or divert. Even if presented with numerous refutations, G•d forbid, their faith remains steadfast in that they received it in an unbroken chain from their

---

[1] This is the implication of the literal translation of the Hebrew syntax of the verse.

forefathers. Still, they never undertook investigation into the existence of G•d. Therefore, the disadvantage of the first type of belief is that their faith is like a commandment done by rote, without apparent reason or understanding.

The second type of belief has a distinctly different advantage in that they know their Creator through extensive investigation. Thus, they are strong due to the knowledge and understanding in their perfect faith. The result is an all encompassing love. However, the disadvantage to this type of belief is that they can or may be easily dissuaded. If people present them with evidence that refutes their conclusions, their faith can be weakened or removed if they are convinced, G•d forbid.

Now we can appreciate that one who has both of these types of belief possesses the firmest faith of all. That is, they rely fully upon their forefathers and have also come to their belief as a result of their own investigation. This is a good and pure faith, and this is why we say, "Our G•d and the G•d of our fathers." This can also explain the verse, "Taste and see that G•d is good"[1] – taste for yourself through investigation and see the conduct of our forefathers.

*Kesser Shem Tov p.19c*

---

[1] Psalms 34:9

1-15 One shouldn't stand to pray without the realization of what is lacking in the upper worlds.

**ONE** should not stand to pray except with koved rosh[1] – with the realization of what is lacking in the head, which are the upper worlds. For example, when a son does not follow the right path, the father suffers and walks around "without a head." On the other hand, when the son is wise and honest, he broadens his father's mind. So, too, with the Congregation of Israel. When they experience lack, it is because the Divine effluence does not pour forth. This outflow is withheld due to a lacking on their part, when they caused a blemish in the upper worlds.

*Likkutei Amarim of*
*R. Menachem Mendel of Vitebsk*

---

[1] Literally, a heavy head. Referring to an attitude of reverence. Mishna *Berachos* 5:1

CHAPTER 2

# SPEECH
# AND PRAYER

2-1 Words begin as thought.

**THE** fundamental principle of speech is that any word you speak initially begins as a thought. Although we live in an immense world, you can only speak with the letters that are in your thoughts; for thoughts are all formed through the combinations of letters.

*Likkutim Yekarim p.17c*

∞

2-2 Speech is part of thought.

**I** heard from my grandfather (the Baal Shem Tov) that speech is one seventh or one tenth of thought, but I don't remember which.

*Degel Machane Ephraim*

∞

2-3 Every word contains the entire world.

**I** heard (from the Baal Shem Tov) that every word contains the entire world.

*Ben Poras Yosef p. 55a*

2-4 G•d sends words to improve the individual and the world.

**WHEN** you make yourself into a chariot for wisdom, your thoughts constantly cling to G•d. As it is written, "to Him shall you cling."[1] The Holy One sends you words that are needed to fix, uplift and improve both you and the world.

*Degel Machane Ephraim, Bereishis*

∞

2-5 Speak with love and awe for G•d.

**WHEN** you speak, you should feel awe, for the realm of speech is the realm of awe. But when you speak with a feeling of love and awe for G•d, you will first feel awe, and then experience immense enthusiasm.

*Tzava'as HaRivash 88*

∞

---

[1] Deuteronomy 10:20

2-6 Both the evil and the good in our life comes from our speech.

**YOUR** soul is mixed with good and evil, in order that it should be free to choose. Therefore, when you speak holy words, they draw down new life from the source of holiness; and when you speak evil words, they draw down new life from the source of evil. So everything in your life, whether good or evil, depends upon your speech.

*Arvei Nachal, Vayishlach*

∞

2-7 Speaking your thoughts causes an equivalent occurrence.

**WHATEVER** you speak is from the realm of speech. Whatever you think is from realm of thought. When you think about good things and put your thoughts into words, they unite the realms of speech and thought and cause good things to happen. But when you speak badly, the words unite the realms of speech and thought and cause bad things to happen, G•d forbid. This is the meaning of, "you choose the tongue of the crafty."[1]

---

[1] Job 15:5

Do not be in the habit of speaking about bad things. Rather, train yourself to think good thoughts and to speak about good things.

*Kesser Shem Tov, part 2 p. 2*

∞

2-8 While speaking spends life-force, each word brings new vitality.

**YOUR** life-force and vitality are the source of your power of speech. As the verse says, "And He blew in his nostrils the breath of life, and the man became a living soul."[1] This can also be translated as, "And the man became a speaking spirit." Thus, when you speak, your words are actually your very life-force, which goes out from you enclothed within your very words. And because your life-force is attached to its source, these very words – as they are spoken – draw to you new life from your Supernal root. In other words, through speaking, you remain alive. That is, while speaking expends your life force, these spoken words themselves draw into you new vitality.

*Arvei Nachal, Vayishlach*

---

[1] Genesis 2:7

2-9 Our world receives life from the speech of the Children of Israel.

**THE** speech of the Children of Israel is from the realm of speech which gives life to the entire world. The thought of the Children of Israel is from the realm of thought. Our world is limited and must receive its life-force from the letters of speech. Those letters form the thoughts of the Children of Israel after first being invested in the seven character traits[1] so that the strength of the life-force is reduced.

This can be understood by considering that it is impossible to look directly at the sun itself. We can, however, look at its light (which emanated from the sun) and derive benefit from it. This is because the strength of the sun's light has been diminished. Were the rays of light from the sun to be as brilliant as the sun itself, they would also be impossible to look at. Thus, it is written: "For a sun and a shield is the L•rd G•d."[2]

*Kesser Shem Tov, part 2 p. 19d*

∞

---

[1] Love, restraint, compassion, conquest, splendor, foundation, and sovereignty; known collectively as the *midot.*
[2] Psalms 84:12

2-10 Speech replenishes our very vitality.

**SPEECH**, which is our very vitality, is from G•d. When you say a good word, it rises up and causes Supernal speech to replenish your vitality. But when you speak evil words, your life-force departs without ascending and it may not be replenished.

*Tzava'as HaRivash 103*

∞

2-11 The life-force that leaves you when you speak is revived by Torah study and prayer.

**WHEN** you speak, your life-force leaves you. By means of the speech of Torah study and prayer, you receive new vitality from your Supernal source. As it says: "The living creatures ran and returned" (Ezekiel 1:14). However, depression does not resonate with holiness, and therefore, speech from a depressed state depletes your life-force, G•d forbid.

*Dudaim ba-Sadeh, B'ha'aloschah*

∞

2-12 Our words should be dedicated to serving G•d.

**THE** Shechinah is in exile because it is the source of all speech. Thus, our speech should be dedicated to serving G•d. Due to our sins, however, we use our words to speak about physical concerns and empty and false values.

*Darchei Tzedek 1:20*

∞

2-13 We only speak about physical desires because of our sins.

**WHY** is the Divine Presence in exile? Because "with the word of G•d, the heavens were made."[1] You must speak solely for G•d's sake to arouse the Supernal speech which created the world, so as to cause it to radiate throughout the creation. However, because of our sins we speak only about physical desires. Even our words of prayer and Torah are filled with foreign thoughts and self-interests. Thus, the Divine Presence is in exile.

*Kisvei Kodesh p. 22b*

---

[1] Psalms 33:6

2-14 The Exile of the Shechinah.

**THE** exile of the Divine Presence is caused by extraneous thoughts being carried within our words.

*Darchei Tzedek, part 1:20*

∞

2-15 To speak your thought illuminates your words.

**"YOU** shall make a window (tzohar) for the ark (teivah)."[1] Tzohar means "light," and teivah means "word." When you want to speak, you must first see to it that your thought illuminates your words, for the Hebrew word "thought" is formed of the letters forming the words chashav mah (meaning 'he thought about what.')[2]

*Toldos Yitzchak, Noach*

∞

---

[1] Genesis 6:16
[2] The letters of the Hebrew word "thought" (*machshava*) can be rearranged as "he thought about what". (*chashav mah*).

2-16 Fear can cause you to tremble from your own speech.

**THERE** is a type of fear that will cause you to tremble at the very words coming out of your mouth, for they are from the World of speech.

*Kesser Shem Tov, part 2 p. 2*

∞

# CHAPTER 3

# PREPARATION FOR PRAYER

3-1 The first words you say in the morning will influence the affect of your prayers.

**BE** careful with every word you say before prayer, for our Sages have prohibited even permissible words, such as greeting someone in the morning.[1] Even that can cause a blemish.

It is well known that the world was created with thought, speech and action. The first level is thought, from which comes speech and from there action. When you awake each morning you are a new creation, as the verse says, "They are new every morning."[2] If your first words are about mundane things (and all the more so, about something forbidden[3]), everything you say later will be similarly influenced – even your prayers and Torah study. Just as speech follows thought, so too, each word follows the previous word.

This concept reflects the teaching of the Zohar[4] and the Arizal[5] that younger siblings must honor the firstborn of their family.[6] For the

---

[1] Talmud, *Berachos* 14a
[2] Lamentations 3:23
[3] Such as profanity, gossip or slander
[4] Zohar 3:83a
[5] Rabbi Isaac Luria (1534 – 1572)
[6] The Arizal teaches that just as children are obligated to respect their parents, so must they respect their firstborn sibling. For the firstborn represents the initial creative act of the parents, from which all subsequent births draw their

firstborn is like the main branch of a tree, whereas later siblings are like offshoots from that main branch. In our case too, you must sanctify and purify your first words and thoughts and attach them to holiness, so that all subsequent words should follow them. Then, when you start to pray, joyful for having sanctified your speech and thoughts, your words of prayer will surely be answered.

*Kesser Shem Tov 20b*

∞

3-2 When you go to perform a mitzvah, do so quickly.

"**RIGHTEOUSNESS** shall go before him, and he will place it on the way of his steps."[1] This verse offers an admonishment. On the way to pray at a shule with a minyan,[2] you might be tempted to stop and to talk to others. Although you eventually fulfill

---

vitality. Thus, Jacob said about Reuben: "Reuben, you are my firstborn, my might and the beginning of my strength ..." (Genesis 49:3).

[1] Psalms 85:14

[2] (lit. number); The quorum of ten necessary for communal prayer.

the mitzvah (Divine commandment) of praying with a minyan, you sinned by not doing it more quickly.

After you leave this world, your punishment is "measure for measure." Your soul must pass over a river on a very narrow bridge. This will be extremely painful to your soul as it feels fear and dread. Yet, the soul must run quickly because a speedy crossing is essential to successfully cross the river. However, in the middle of the bridge, G•d sends an angel to block the soul. This is the same angel that was created by the Divine command-ment[1] which you went to perform but stopped on the way. At that time, the angel you caused to be created had suffered because your thoughts while stopping to talk before performing the mitzvah, created the angel's soul and the actual performance of the mitzvah created its body. However, because you delayed in creating the angel's body when you stopped to talk, the angel will now stop you in the middle of the bridge. Preventing the soul from crossing causes it to become extremely frightened.

Thus, the plain meaning of "righteousness shall go before him" is that all of your actions will precede you after leaving this world. Knowing this, make sure that when you go to do a mitzvah, do so quickly so that "he will place it on the way of his

---

[1] Every Divine commandment you perform an angel is created.

steps." That is to say, your soul will not be hindered when crossing the bridge over the river.

*Tzava'as HaRivash, p.14a*

∞

3-3 G•d rewards based on a person's love for a mitzvah.

"**AND** Yours my G•d, is kindness; for You repay each man according to his deeds."[1] The Baal Shem Tov once explained this verse with the following story. There was once a harsh judgment against the Congregation of Israel on Yom Kippur. The Accusing Angel was not critical of the wicked, but of the G•d-fearing, who pray each day in synagogue. The angel gave the example that on their way to pray at the synagogue, they may see a wagon load of wood for sale and stop to bargain over the price. The result is that they come late to prayer services and miss Borchu[2] and Kedusha,[3] all for the small savings they receive from the seller.

---

[1] Psalms 62:13
[2] Short prayer said with minyan before blessings preceding kriyas Shema.
[3] Short prayer said in the repetition of the Amidah.

None of the defending angels could refute this. Fortunately, he (Rabbenu Baal Shem Tov) came to the Congregation of Israel's defense. True, he agreed that a reward for a mitzvah can be lost for some trifling amount of money before it is performed; however, after it has been fulfilled, no Jewish person would sell the mitzvah for the greatest fortune, even the most foolhardily of them.

With this argument, the Baal Shem Tov sweetened the harsh judgments. This is the meaning of, "And Yours my G•d, is kindness; for You repay each man according to his deeds." That is, a person is rewarded according to the love he has for the mitzvah after he performs it, not necessarily before.

*Degel Machane Reuven 59*

∞

3-4 Praying before sunrise to annul the Divine judgments.

**MAKE** sure that you always pray before sunrise, both in the summer and in the winter. That is, you should recite most of the prayers, until just before kriyas Shema,[1] before sunrise. The difference between praying before or after sunrise is as great as is the east from the west. The reason is that before sunrise, one can still annul Divine Judgments, as is alluded to in the verses, "He has set in them [in the Heavens] a tent for the sun ... which is like a bridegroom coming from his bridal canopy, rejoicing like a strong man rejoicing to run the course ... there is nothing hidden from its heat."[2] Do not read the word as "heat" (chamaso) but as "wrath" (chemaso). For when the sun is already out, it is impossible to hide from the Divine Judgments that come from the angels of wrath.

Praying before sunrise is extremely important and is not to be taken lightly. The Baal Shem Tov was so careful with this that he would pray alone if he did not have a sunrise minyan.

*Tzava'as HaRivash, p.3a*

∞

---

[1] Reading of Shema; Deuteronomy 6:4-9 and 11:13-21 and Numbers 15:37-41.
[2] Psalms 19:5-7

3-5 Learning Zohar before the daily prayers.

**THE** Baal Shem Tov instructed his disciples to learn a passage of Zohar before each of the daily prayers.

*Likkutei Torah 7*

∞

3-6 Strengthen yourself before praying by first reciting psalms or studying Torah.

**STRENGTHEN** yourself before praying so that you will, at least, have no foreign thoughts, and ideally, will pray with deep devotion. You can do this by first reciting psalms or studying Torah, and then pray amidst those words. This will give you presence of mind. On the other hand, for some people, saying a lot of Psalms or studying Torah decreases their ability to concentrate. Thus, it says: "One gives a lot and another a little, as long as a person's heart is directed to heaven."[1]

*Traditional Chassidic Source*

∞

---

[1] Talmud *Menachos* 110a, *Berachos* 5b

3-7 Do not recite too many psalms before you pray, so as not to become too weak to recite the obligatory prayers.

**DO** not recite too many Psalms before you pray, so as not to weaken your body. By exerting yourself too much before prayer, you will not be able to recite the obligatory prayers[1] of the daily prayer services with a strong spiritual attachment.

Accordingly, first recite the main parts of the daily prayer with deep devotion. Then, if G•d gives you more strength, you can say Psalms or the Song of Songs afterwards. On Yom Kippur too, say the prayers of the machzor[2] before Ne'ilah[3] in a state of katnus[4], so that you can pray the Ne'ilah prayer with devotion.

*Tzava'as HaRivash 38*

∞

---

[1] Hymns of Praise, the Shema and the Amidah
[2] Specialized form of the siddur for holiday use
[3] Concluding prayer service said on Yom Kippur
[4] Spiritual smallness

3-8 Contemplating before and after prayer.

**THE** early chassidim would begin an hour before prayer and conclude an hour after prayer. Before prayer, they would contemplate their own lowliness and the greatness of the Creator. After prayer, they would contemplate on how they did not pray with enough intensity or kavanah[1] before the King of Kings and how their prayers accomplished nothing.

*Ohr Yisroel*

∞

3-9 Before prayer, bring yourself to a state of awe before G•d.

**WHEN** you want to pray, first bring yourself to a state of awe before G•d, for this is the gate to enter the chamber of the Blessed One.[2] Say in your heart, "To Whom do I want to attach myself? To Him Who created all the worlds with His word, and Who enlivens and sustains them!" You should meditate on His greatness and exaltation. Then you

---

[1] Intention
[2] See Talmud *Shabbat* 31b

can enter the supernal worlds. Tzava'as HaRivash 66

∞

3-10 Plead with G•d to give you a sign before prayer.

"**ASK** for a sign (os) from the L•rd your G•d."[1] You should plead with the Holy One to give you a letter.[2] The letters that you speak in Torah study and prayer should be of those that are attached to the L•rd. That is, you should merit attaching them to their source in G•d.          Me'or Einayim, Ki Sisa

∞

---

[1] Isaiah 7:11
[2] The Hebrew os means both "sign" and "letter."

# CHAPTER 4

# THE ESSENCE OF PRAYER

## A. Prayer for the Sake of G•d

4-a1. All of our prayers should be for the sake of G•d, and not for our own benefit.

"**DO** not be like servants who serve their master in order to receive a reward; rather be like servants who serve their master without the intent to receive a reward."[1] There is another version of this teaching, "be like servants who serve their master in order not to receive a reward." Both versions are correct and describe two different levels of worship, one higher than the other.

"Without the intent to receive a reward" is the correct and proper form of worship. Your prayers should be solely for the sake of G•d, regardless of whether or not you receive the object of your prayers. Indeed, everything you do should be for the sake of G•d, and not for your benefit in any way whatsoever.

However, there is another, higher level of prayer. For instance, a certain person has a deep and burning desire to speak with the king. The king issues a decree that he will grant any request that is made of him. When this person who longs to speak to the king presents his request, he is actually worried that the king will fulfill it, for then

---

[1] Mishna *Avot* 1:3

he will have nothing more to speak about with the king. Rather, he prefers that the king not fulfill his request, so that he can come before the king and speak to him again.

This is the meaning of, "A prayer for a poor man when he enwraps himself and pours out his tale of woe before G•d"[1]. That is, his prayer is that he can pour out his tale of woe before G•d. This is also alluded to in the Talmud in the story of Shmuel HaKatan.[2] This is the meaning of: "in order not to receive a reward." Degel Machane Ephraim

---

[1] Psalms 102:1

[2] Talmud *Ta'anis* 25b Once, in a period of drought, Shmuel HaKatan declared a public fast. The rains fell that same day, although after sunset. (This was considered late, as another story in the Talmud tells of the rain falling immediately in the morning.) The people assumed that it was because G•d desired to hear the prayers of the congregation the entire day. Shmuel HaKatan, however, rejected this assumption.

However, as stated in the Zohar (2:15a): "Once, the world needed rain. Rabbi Eliezer came and decreed forty fasts, but the rain did not come. He prayed, but the rain still did not come. Rabbi Akiva rose to pray. He said, "Who makes the wind blow?" The wind started to blow. He said, "Who makes the rains fall?" The rains started to fall. Rabbi Eliezer became dejected, but Rabbi Akiva looked in his face and stood before him. "I will tell you a parable," he said. "What is this like? Rabbi Eliezer is like the beloved of a king. The king is pleased when he comes before him too quickly. The king does not grant him his request speedily, in order that he not leave him. This is because he is pleased to talk with him. But I am like a servant of the king that makes a request. He does not want me to enter the palace gates, and moreover, not to talk to him. Therefore the king says, 'Fulfill his request quickly, and do

4-a2. Different levels of prayer.

**THERE** are many aspects of prayer, one higher than the other. On the lowest level, you pray for your own needs. This is the level of the world, as it is written, "All flesh is grass, and all their goodness is like the flowers of the field,"[1] and "Their acts of kindness are only for themselves."[2]

The next level is to pray to fill that which is lacking in the Shechinah. Indeed, by rectifying the Supernal Source, the deficiency below, in our physical world, is also filled – for the Above and the below are one. However, you should not intend to repair both Above and below, for this is like "uprooting the shoots"[3] and creates a division.

I also heard an explanation of the Talmud's statement, "There are things that stand at the height of the world, yet people belittle them."[4] The meaning is that the effects of prayer become realized Above, in the heights of the world, and not always below. Therefore, people belittle prayer and

---

not let him in.' Thus, Rabbi Eliezer is a beloved of the king, and I am a servant. The King wants to talk to you (Rabbi Eliezer) the entire day and not have you leave. But the king does not want me to enter the gates of the palace." Rabbi Eliezer was placated.

[1] Isaiah 40:6
[2] Tikunei Zohar, *Tikun* 30, p.73b
[3] A reference to heresy.
[4] A reference to prayer.

imagine that their supplications are worthless. But this is not so.

There is yet an even higher level; when you do not even demand that Supernal rectifications be accomplished, for there is a danger in that as well. The story of Rabbi Yosef d'LeReina is proof.[1] Therefore, the best thing for a wise person is simply to pray over whatever happens, and let the Master of Desire do as He knows best. This is the most exalted level – a service that is not for the sake of receiving repayment.

*Toldos Yaakov Yosef p. 144b*

∞

4-a3. When a person prays only to speak to G•d, all his other needs are encompassed in his simple request.

**"A** prayer for a poor man when he enwraps himself and pours out his speech before G•d."[2] One might think that the verse should be, "a prayer from a poor man"? The Baal Shem Tov explained

---

[1] A fifteenth century kabbalist who tried to force the coming of Moshiach but failed and caused the Spanish exile instead.
[2] Psalms 102:1

the reason for the wording of the verse with a parable.

There was once a great and compassionate king who proclaimed that he would grant every request that was made of him. Some people asked for silver and gold, others for positions of authority. One wise man, however, asked to find grace in the king's eyes and to be allowed to speak with him three times a day. The king was pleased with his request, seeing that he preferred the king's words to gold and silver. So the king decreed that whenever the wise man would enter his inner chamber to speak with him, he should be led past the king's treasuries and be allowed to take whatever he wants.

Now, the king is best called a "poor man," for he really has nothing: everything is under the supervision of his treasurer. Thus it says, "A prayer for a poor man." Meaning, this person beseeches and prays to the King of Kings, the Poor One, that he should be allowed to speak to Him. "When he is enwrapped" means that his requests are all enwrapped by the treasures of the King of Kings. The reason is this: when he prays that he should be able speak to the Him himself, everything else he needs is automatically included in this simple request.                Toldos Yaakov Yosef p. 178c

4-a4. G•d longs for the words of prayer.

**"WHEN** I am in distress, I call upon the L•rd; yes, I cry out to my G•d; out of His temple He hears my voice, and my cry comes before Him in His ears."[1]

Speech is called a temple. You should pray only for your words to come before G•d. Then, all the heavenly gatekeepers will leave you alone. For example, when a simple villager carries the king's seal, though he is unfit to enter before the king, the guards rush him in. This is because the king longs for his seal, and the guards want him to have it as quickly as possible.

So too, G•d longs for the words of prayer. This is the meaning of, "out of His temple He hears my voice."

*Ohr Torah, Likkutim p. 54a*

∞

4-a5. Every word, gesture, step and action influences what is Above.

**A** person's many sins keep him from serving G•d. In his lowly state, he cannot believe that his

---

[1] Psalms 18:7

prayers and Torah study could draw Divine blessings into all the worlds, to the extent that even the angels are nourished. Were he to believe that, he would serve G•d with joy and awe and would carefully recite each letter and word of prayer. Moreover, he would remember that which is written, "When you lie between the sheepfolds (sefasayim)."[1] That is, G•d watches a person's lips (sefasayim) and kisses them when they say words of Torah and prayer with reverence and love. Who would not be filled with fear and dread upon realizing that the great and awesome King watches the lips, even those of a person who is "despised and forsaken of men?"[2]

Our Sages have said, "The humility of Rabbi Zechariah caused the destruction of the Temple."[3] A person should realize that he is a "ladder standing upon the earth, with his head reaching Heaven"[4] and that his every word, gesture, step and action make its mark Above. Then, he will make sure that his deeds are all for the sake of G•d.

But when he thinks, "Am I really significant enough to damage or repair that which is Above and below? Are all my deeds really recorded in

---

[1] Psalms 68:14
[2] Isaiah 53:3
[3] Talmud *Gittin* 56a
[4] Genesis 28:12

heaven?" he will feel unaccountable for his thoughts, speech and actions. He will find himself saying, "I will have peace."[1] But this is not true; for through our good deeds, we actually cling to G•d. As it is written: "You shall go in His ways."[2] That is, our compassionate actions below arouse the attribute of compassion in all of the worlds above.

Thus, the phrase: "Know what is above from you,"[3] can be interpreted as meaning "Know that what is Above, is from you yourself, from the various emotions that you feel."

*Toldos Yaakov Yosef p. 181c*

∞

---

[1] Deuteronomy 29:18
[2] Deuteronomy 29:9
[3] Mishna *Avos* 2:1

## B. The Repair of Malchut

4-b1. The essence of prayer is to sweeten the Judgments of Malchut[1] in Binah[2].

**THE** essence of prayer is to bind the Judgments of Malchut, and to sweeten the Judgments at their root, which is Binah.

*Ben Poras Yosef p. 116b*

∞

4-b2. The purpose of prayer is to unite Chochmah[3] with Malchut.

**THE** purpose of prayer is to unite the Hebrew letter yud, which is Chochmah, with the Hebrew letter hey, which is Malchut – prayer – by means of the voice, which is Y-K-V-K,[4] and one's thoughts, which is Binah. This is the mystery of [the Divine

---

[1] Malchut is the tenth sephirah, and the final emotive attribute within Creation.
[2] Understanding: the ability to infer one thing from another; the eight sefirah in ascending order, characterized by suprarational perception.
[3] Wisdom; the ninth sephirah in ascending order; the seminal spark or flash of insight that implicitly contains all ramifications thereof; down to the most physical details; the root of intellect.
[4] The Tetragrammaton.

Names] E-H-Y-K, Y-K-V-K, A-D-N-I. It is called "prayer," for it joins the human being to his Creator.[1]

*Likutim Yikarim, p. 4b*

∞

4-b3. The purpose of prayer is to unite Chochmah with Malchut.

**THE** purpose of prayer is to unite Chochmah with Malchut by means of the voice and thoughts.

*Likkutim Yikarim p. 4b*

∞

4-b4 Prayer can change a judgment from bad to good.

**NACHMANIDES**[2] asks about the nature of prayer: How can it change a Divine decree?[3] Can

---

[1] The root of the word "prayer" – *tefilah* – share the same root letters as the word *naftuli* (as in *Genesis 30:8*), one meaning of which is "a close adhesion." (See Rashi on this verse.)

[2] Ramban, *Rabbi Moshe ben Nahman* (1194ce - 1270ce)

[3] See also the commentary "HaKosev" on *Ein Yaakov, Berachos,* chapter 5.

G•d's Will be changed?[1] If a person was praying for himself, we could understand how His Will can be changed. For just as he changed his own behavior from bad to good, so G•d's decree can be changed from bad to good. But this principle should not apply to prayers offered on someone else's behalf.

The Baal Shem Tov explained, in the name of his Heavenly teacher,[2] that prayer sweetens the judgment of Malchut, which is called Din[3], in its root in Binah. When you pray in this way for a friend, you bind them to their Supernal root, and they become a different person.

To explain this further, it is known that the Divine decree is a drop of seed in the womb of Malchut, and that it is composed of letters. As the Talmud says: "Betzalel knew how to combine the letters that went into the creation of heaven and earth."[4] Now, the King of Kings surely does not carry out His decrees Himself. He appoints an emissary who makes use of the word-combinations that convey the decree. However, the emissary can

---

[1] Seeing that G•d's Will is part of His Essence, since He is unchangeable, so His Will is unchangeable.

[2] The prophet, Achiya HaShiloni.

[3] Judgement

[4] Berachos 55a.

rearrange the first letters of the words so that they imply something else.[1]

Now the Tzaddik, who is the emissary of the Shechinah,[2] who knows how to sweeten the judgments and bind the drop that is in Malchut to Binah, thus transforming it into something else.

*Katones Passim, p. 47b*

∞

4-b6 Changing G•d's mind.

**THE** Ramban asked how prayer can "change" G•d's mind. The Baal Shem Tov answered, in the name of his teacher,[3] that the point of prayer is to sweeten Malchut in its root — binding a person there in its root through his intentions. In that place, they are a different person. The Baal Shem Tov further explained that every Supernal judgment

---

[1] The Baal Shem Tov here specifies recombining the first letters of words to change the meaning of the decree. However, in other lessons, he speaks about different types of letter combinations that can alter the decree that descends from above.

[2] The Divine Presence; the Sefirah of Malchut of Knesset Israel, the collective of the Jewish souls. Literally, the "Matron," a phrase from the Zohar for the Shechinah.

[3] Achiyah HaShiloni

is composed of letters, which the courier is able to rearrange. For instance, through prayer, the reish (Hebrew letter) is moved before the tzadi, so that trouble -- tzara, – צרה is changed to desire -- ratza, רצה.

*Darchei Tzedek, p. 53*

∞

CHAPTER 5

# PRAYING FOR THE DIVINE PRESENCE

## A. Praying from knowledge

5-a1 Praying for the needs of the Shechinah.

**TZADDIKIM** are the messengers of the Matron.[1] Through their own suffering and deprivation, they know the privations of the Shechinah and pray for its needs to be fulfilled, uniting it with the Holy One. This is the greatness of prayer.[2]

This answers the age-old question as to why we need to pray, since G•d surely knows our needs. It is written, "He tests the loins and the heart"[3]. Prayer is for a higher purpose. When we realize that our own lacking derives from the privations Above and pray for the Shechinah's needs to be fulfilled, our own needs will also be assuaged. However, you should never think about your own needs, only the needs of the Shechinah.

*Tzafnah Paneach p. 50c*

---

[1] A reference to the *Shechinah*
[2] See also Degel Machane Ephraim, B'Chukosai: What is it in a person that feels pleasure or pain? It is his soul and his life-force, for when these depart, he feels nothing. Now, this life-force is united – with the source of all life and creation, which is G•d. When you remember this and think about your source, which is the Shechinah, and pray for it, you create a complete unification. This is the meaning of, "Tzaddikim are the messengers of the Matron." Through their own deprivation and suffering, they know and pray for any lacking in the Shechinah.
[3] Jeremiah 11:20

5-a2 Praying for the Shechinah's suffering to subside.

**A** wise person knows that all of his own suffering also causes pain to the Divine Presence, as it says in the Talmud, "When a person is in pain, what does the Shechinah say? 'My head hurts me! My arm hurts me!'"[1] Thus, if the wise person prays for the Shechinah's suffering to subside, their own suffering will abate as well.

*Toldos Yaakov Yosef, Beshalach*

∞

5-a3 Beseech G•d to unite the Shechinah with the Holy One.

**"HEAR** me, pursuers of righteousness,[2] you who seek G•d. Look at the rock from where you were hewn and the pit from where you were dug. Look at Abraham your father, and Sarah your mother, who bore you. He was one, alone, when I

---

[1] Talmud *Sanhedrin* 46a
[2] "Righteousness" – *tzedek* – is another term for Malchut-Shechinah.

called him, and I blessed him and made him many."[1]

The "pursuers of righteousness" are those who pursue faith. They are the seekers of G•d. If you want to know faith and to be attached to this righteousness, do not look at it directly, as do others who cause themselves to die. Rather, "look at the rock from where you were hewn."[2]

It has been explained that all requests should be on behalf of the Shechinah. This is called prayer, for the Divine Presence beseeches and prays to G•d for its needs. Now, whatever a person lacks is caused by a lack in the Shechinah, and in praying for that lack to be rectified Above, a healing is necessarily drawn below.

However, "the heart knows its own bitterness"[3] and that not all times are equal. If a person experiences some great pain, G•d forbid, he might pray for himself without realizing that the Shechinah is also suffering. In fact, it would have been much better for him to pray for the Shechinah instead. In the middle of prayer, a person might try to forget his prayerful appeal and to beseech for the Shechinah alone, but without truly being able to overcome his own pain. By professing that his

---

[1] Isaiah 51:1
[2] *Zohar* 3:222b.
[3] Proverbs 14:10

66

prayer is for the Shechinah without truly negating his own needs, he may actually be pushed away entirely – for, indeed, G•d knows what is true. Therefore, the advice is to pray simply on whichever level possible. Simply keep your mouth and heart together, for "a speaker of lies will not be established before My eyes."[1]

The lowest level of creation is called Malchut by itself. This, however, is not the case when the Shechinah is truly united with the Holy One through prayer. Then, they are attached to Zeir Anpin.[2] This is not the case with Malchut alone. Only when Malchut is united with the Holy One does a person also become attached to the true source. Therefore, "Pursuers of justice, who search for G•d" are the righteous messengers of the Shechinah. It is as though they beseech G•d for righteousness itself to unite the Shechinah with the Holy One.

*Toldos Yaakov Yosef p. 100d*

∞

---

[1] Psalms 101:7

[2] lit. "small countenance; The collection of Divine attributes excluding Malchut (might).

5-a4 Praying for food or clothing causes a Supernal outflow of food or clothing to be drawn down on Tzaddikim.

**TZADDIKIM** are the messengers of the Divine Presence. Moreover, from their own privations, such as for food or clothing, they clearly perceive that which is lacking Above. They pray for it to be filled. They do not pray for their own sake at all.

Nevertheless, when an ordinary person prays for food or clothing, a Supernal outflow of food or clothing is also drawn down for tzaddikim, whose prayers are only for spiritual needs and never for physical or material ones.

*Ben Poras Yosef p. 23b*

∞

## B. Prayer

5-b1 The Baal Shem Tov cured people through the uplifting of the Shechinah.

**ALL** of a person's needs, such as health and livelihood, are called "limbs of the Divine Presence" for whatever is lacking below is correspondingly lacking Above. Thus, you must pray only to repair what is Above and not at all for your personal needs. Then, as a direct consequence of your purposeful objective, that which is lacking below will be fixed. The Baal Shem Tov cured people only by unifying and uplifting the Shechinah. As a result, the lower world was fixed as well.

*Me'or Einayim, Naso*

∞

5-b2 Pray over the lack in the Shechinah

**ONE** should not rise to pray except with koved rosh.[1] That is, do not pray for something that you personally lack because your prayer may not be accepted. Rather, pray over the heaviness in the

---

[1] Literally, a heavy head. Referring to an attitude of reverence. Mishna *Berachos* 5:1

"head"[1] – for whatever you lack is also missing in the Shechinah. By His design, a person is a part of G•d's Oneness. What is missing in the part, or any of the parts, is also lacking in the whole, and the whole feels the deficiency of the part. Therefore, you should pray over the lack in the whole, i.e., the Shechinah.

*Tzava'as HaRivash 73*

∞

5-b3 Praying to fulfill your own material desires will create a division between yourself and G•d.

**THE** Shechinah is called "prayer," as it is written: "And I[2] am prayer.[3]" When you pray, do so with the intent to unite the Shechinah with its Partner[4], without considering your personal benefit, G•d forbid. For of this it is said, "The L•rd has delivered me into the hands of those I cannot withstand."[5] That is, if you pray to fulfill your own material desires, you create a division between

---

[1] A reference to the *Shechinah*
[2] Here, "I" refers to *Malchut*.
[3] Psalms 109:4
[4] A reference to G•d.
[5] Lamentations 1:14

yourself and G•d for you have brought materialism into the spiritual realm. You will not be answered at all.

*Tzafnah Paneach p. 2c*

∞

5-b4 Forget yourself completely and pray only for the good of the Shechinah.

**YOU** must think of yourself as nothing, forget yourself completely and pray only for the good of the Shechinah. Through self-abnegation, you can attain the realm of thought, which transcends time – where everything is equal. This is the meaning of the statement, "'Why do they cry to Me?'[1] – 'to Me' specifically, for the matter depends upon Atik."[2] They had to abandon themselves completely and forget their own danger in order to enter the realm

---

[1] Exodus 14:15

[2] Zohar 2:48a. When the Jewish people stood before the Red Sea, they cried out to G•d. He responded to Moshe our teacher, "Why do they cry out to Me? Speak to the Children of Israel and tell them to travel on." It is explained that their prayers were to a lower level of Divine manifestation – "to Me" – whereas the redemption depended upon the revelation of *Atik*, which is the most recondite level of Divinity and above all duality and difference.

71

of thought where everything is equal.[1] However, when you are attached to this physical world, you are attached to the duality of good and evil. How, then, can you rise above corporeality to absolute Oneness? So, too, when you consider yourself as something and pray for your own needs, G•d is unable to clothe Himself in you, for G•d is infinite, and no vessel can contain Him. This is not the case if you consider yourself as nothing.

*Likkutei Amarim p. 18c*

∞

5-b5 Pray by saying the letters and the words simply and understanding their meaning.

**THERE** are people who sing the words of prayer. They even have specific melodies for the different prayer sections. They imagine that this is a holy way to serve G•d because it will generate enthusiasm in them, and that through this they will please G•d. However, their way is foolish. It is empty and false worship. They walk in darkness and have not yet come upon the path of truth.

---

[1] By transcending their own concerns and reaching the realm of thought, the sea turned into dry land, allowing them to pass though since on that level of unity, everything is equal.

The true path is as follows: A person must strip himself of all physicality during prayer until it seems that he is not in this world at all. He should say the letters and words simply, attaching his thoughts to the holy letters and understanding their meaning. Then, suddenly, a great and powerful fire of Supernal fear and love will ignite in him. This is the true way in serving G•d.

*Rabbi Aharon of Zidichov*

∞

5-b6 Asking the letters of prayer to help you speak the words with true and selfless intent.

**YOU** must actually ask the letters of prayer – the secret Divinity that exists within them – to help you speak the words with true and selfless intent. This sweetens the Gevurah[1] at its root.

*Degel Machane Ephraim, Beshalach*

∞

---

[1] Strict judgment

## C. Fixing

5-c1 When we acknowledge His greatness and dominion, His trait of Malchut is complete.

**WE** recite "For the sake of the unification of the Holy One and His Shechinah"[1] in order to unite Tiferet[2] and Malchut.[3] In this way, the Holy One becomes proud[4] of Malchut for this level corresponds to speech and enlivens the entire world. As it is written, "With the word of G•d, the heavens were made"[5] and "You give life to them all."[6] G•d's words constantly enliven the universe. When a person performs a commandment, the Holy One takes delight in Malchut – in His speech – which is within the worlds. This is the concept of the union, the unification of the Holy One and his Shechinah – G•d should take great joy in His Kingship that is within the world, and He should reveal His Kingship so that everyone will recognize that He is the

---

[1] This formula was established by the Arizal to be recited before each prayer and the performance of certain mitzvot.
[2] (lit. beauty); The Divine attribute of compassion.
[3] This union is the principle mystical achievement of our prayers and mitzvos. It brings about a higher union between Chochmah and Binah, which engenders Divine effluence in the world.
[4] An alternate connotation of tiferet.
[5] Psalms 33:6
[6] Nehemiah 9:6

Ruler of the world. This is a great delight for the Holy One.

The revelation of His Kingship is from our side. In other words, His Creation of mankind is the prerequisite. Then, when we acknowledge His greatness and dominion, Malchut is complete, for "there is no King without a people." On account of the people, His Kingship is revealed. This gives G•d great pleasure.

*Likkutim Yikarim p. 4a*

∞

5-c2 When we pray for G•d's sake, there are no obstructions at all.

**G•D** relates to our prayers for material needs, such as: "Heal us and we shall be healed," "Bless us with a good year," etc., like a father who loves his child and wants to fulfill even his most frivolous desires. For it is the nature of one who is good to do good.

G•d's only thinks how to bestow material blessings on the Children of Israel, who are called His children. Prayer, then, draws down sustenance and effluence to all the worlds — even to the material world — to satisfy G•d's longing. Thus, prayers [for the sake of G•d] are accepted immediately. Whereas Heaven scrutinizes our prayers for ourselves to see if we are worthy. When we pray for G•d's sake, there are no obstructions whatsoever.

*Kedushas Levi, Likutim Shonim, p. 509*

∞

5-c3 All of your requests should be that G•d is fulfilled.

**IT** is known that "In all their afflictions, He was afflicted" (Isaiah 63:9), and "I am with him in trouble" (Psalms 91:15). Yet, it states in the Tikkunei Zohar: "They cry out like dogs, but there is no one to wake in repentance to break out of their prison cell."[1] For the main repentance must be for G•d's honor, which means rectifying and removing the agony caused by our sins. In all that you request, have in mind the honor of the Shechinah, i.e., that G•d's [requests] should be fulfilled. This is the meaning of: "May G•d fulfill all of your requests" (Psalms 20:6). That is, all of your requests should be that G•d is fulfilled.

---

[1] Tikkunei Zohar 7.

When your intentions are only for the sake of G•d, you cause the Shechinah to ascend, and create a Unification with G•d.

*Mevaser Tzedek, Chukas*

∞

5-c4 All words should be dedicated to G•d.

**THE** Shechinah is in exile because She is the source of all words, and all words should be devoted to G•d. However, due to our sins, we use those very words to speak about physical concerns and empty and false values.

*Darchei Tzedek 1:20*

∞

5-c5 Speak for G•d's sake alone to cause the Supernal speech to radiate throughout all the worlds.

**WHY** is the Divine Presence in exile? Because "with the word of G•d, the heavens were made" (Psalms 33:6). You must speak for G•d's sake alone; that is, in order to arouse the Supernal speech which created the worlds, to radiate throughout all the worlds. However, because of our sins, we routinely discuss only our physical desires. Even our words of prayer and Torah are filled with foreign thoughts and self-interest. Thus speech is in exile.

*Kisvei Kodesh, p. 22b*

∞

5-c7 The effect of the exile of the Divine Presence.

**THE** exile of the Divine Presence means that foreign thoughts "ride" upon your words.

*Darchei Tzedek, part 1, §20*

∞

# CHAPTER 6

# EMOTIONS IN PRAYER

6-1 Joyous prayer is certainly more pleasing to G•d than depressed and tearful prayers.

**JOYOUS** prayer is certainly more pleasing to G•d, blessed be He, than depressed and tearful prayers. For example, a poor man who entreats the king with great sobs and cries will still only receive a little. However, when a minister joyfully praises the king before him and then makes his request, the king will bestow upon him bountifully, as befits the minister's stature.

*Tzava'as HaRivash, 107*

∞

6-2 G•d is not critical when you read the words of the Torah with love and passion.

**IF** you read the Torah and sees the lights in its letters, though you don't fully understand the cantillation marks[1] and pronounce the words incorrectly, G•d is not critical of you, since you read the words with love and passion. This is like a child who requests something from his father who loves him dearly. Though the child stutters and doesn't get the words out right, his father doesn't insist

---

[1] Diacritical symbol attached to a letter or a word.

that he say them correctly. This is as our Sages have said [on the verse]: "His banner over me is love" (Song of Songs 2:4). "Do not read the words as 'His banner over me is love' (diglo alai ahava); rather, read it as 'over the mistakes I make, there is love' (laglago alai ahava)."[1]

*Likutim Yikarim, p. 1*

∞

6-3 There are times when you should serve G•d solely with your thoughts.

**THERE** are times when you should serve G•d with your soul alone; that is, with your thoughts. Your body should then remain still so as not to weaken your body from using it with extraneous movements.

*Tzava'as HaRivash, 104*

∞

---

[1] Midrash Rabbah, Shir HaShirim 2:3.

6-4 You can prayer with love, awe and tremendous passion without moving at all.

**AT** times, you can say your prayers with love, awe and tremendous passion without moving at all, so that to someone else, it appears that you are merely saying the words of prayer without deveikut at all. Because you are then deeply attached to G•d, you can serve Him with your soul alone, with a great and powerful love [of G•d].

This form of worship is better and goes faster and with deeper attachment to G•d than prayers that are outwardly visible in the limbs; for the kelipot[1] cannot attach themselves to this prayer because it is completely internal.

*Tzava'as HaRivash, 105*

∞

6-5 When you pray with the love of G•d in your heart, the words leave your mouth by themselves.

**SOMETIMES**, you can pray extremely quickly because of the love of G•d that burns in your heart.

---

[1] "Impure shells." In this case, alluding to extraneous thoughts.

Then, the words leave your mouth by themselves.

Tzava'as HaRivash, 36

∞

6-6 You should increase your enthusiasm as you pray.

**WE** recite Hodu[1] in the prayer service between the Sacrificial Section and the Verses of Song,[2] and not in the middle of the latter,[3] because the Sacrificial Section is in Asiyah,[4] the Verses of Song is in Yetzirah,[5] and the blessing "who forms light" is in Beriyah.[6] This is the mystery of the angels called Ophanim, Chayot and Seraphim.[7] In Asiyah they are called Ophanim, from the word

---

[1] The section of the prayers beginning with Psalms 105:1: "O give thanks to G•d, call upon His name; make His deeds known among the peoples."

[2] In the morning prayers.

[3] As had been the custom of European Jews before the Baal Shem Tov, and still today in *nusach ashkenaz*.

[4] lit. deed); The final level in the Divine creative process which includes the physical universe.

[5] Yetzirah: (lit. formation); The realm of spiritual existence in which the limited nature of the created beings takes on form and definition.

[6] (lit. creation); The realm of spiritual existence which represents the first beginnings of a consciousness of self.

[7] Various types of angels. See Ezekiel 1.

"wheel,"[1] for these angels clamor[2] and desire to be bound Above. They also reflect the mystery of the nefesh,[3] which implies gain or addition, for they long to gain additional Divine effluence and vitality. Higher than these are the angels of Yetzirah. A greater degree of supernal life reaches them; thus, they are called Chayot ("Living Creatures"). The angels of Beriyah are still higher, and their desire burns even stronger to bind themselves Above. Thus, they are called Seraphim (Fiery Angels).

Now, a human being is a microcosm of the world above. When you wake in the morning, you are devoid of fear of G•d. When you recite the Sacrificial section, you purify yourself[4] and enter the mystery of Asiyah. Then, you are like an Ophan that yearns to move and bind itself to G•d. How do you do this? By saying the Verses of Song. For you become more enthusiastic in these verses than in the Sacrificial section. However, you must begin on a lower level. Therefore, Hodu is first recited, which is merely a collection of verses and not the Verses of Song themselves. This helps you recite the Verses of Praise with greater enthusiasm. Then you become more enthusiastic, which corresponds to

---

[1] *Ophan* (pl. *Ophanayim*) is another word for "wheel."
[2] *Golalim*, literally, "roll over."
[3] Soul
[4] See Zohar 3:120b.

the Chayot.[1] In the blessing, "who forms light," he attains an even greater level of ecstasy, and reaches the level of the Seraphim.

*Likutey Yikarim, p. 4c*

∞

6-7 To elevate your words, speak with fear and love.

**WHEN** you speak, think about "allusion, voice and speech." Speak with fear and love, and imagine that the World of Speech is emanating through your mouth. Then you will elevate your words.

*Kesser Shem Tov II, p. 4b*

∞

6-8 Pray for the sake of the words because the words desire to be bound to thought.

**THIS** is the meaning of praying "for the sake of the Name."[1] That is, pray for the sake of the

---

[1] This word can also be read as *chiyot*, which means life and vitality.

words, for the words themselves long and desire to be bound to thought. When a person speaks with love and fear, his voice and words delight in each other. Thought watches over this, like a father who delights in his child. For thought longs to enter into voice, in order to come into words.

*Likutim Amarim, p. 18b*

∞

6-9 Try to say at least one word of prayer with love and fear, for that arouses all the angels to sing to G•d.

**WHEN** a person speaks with love and fear, the Shechinah desires their words, like a mother who longs to hear her son speak with wisdom, so that her husband should admire her too. Likewise, when through a person's efforts the words are

---

[1] Usually meaning, "for the sake of the thing itself," such as, Torah study for the sake of studying, prayer for the sake of praying; i.e. without ulterior motives. However, the Chasidic movement gave this term a new meaning: *"Leshema"* – "For the sake of the Name" (literally "to the Name"), that is, for the sake of G•d's Presence in creation. At times, the word is broken into two: *le'shem hey* – ה לשם': "For the sake of the letter *hey*," representing *Malchut* and the Shechinah. In the present case, for the sake of the Name is a reference to prayer, which also corresponds to the Shechinah.

beautified and rise Above, a great splendor is born and the angels declare: "Who is like Your people Israel, a unique nation in the earth" (1 Chronicles 17:21).

Try to say [at least] one word of prayer with love and fear, for that arouses all the angels to sing to G•d. For when you serve G•d, you arouse all of the worlds to serve G•d as well.

*Kesser Shem Tov, part 2, p. 5a*

∞

6-10 Be fearful when you speak.

**YOU** should be fearful when you speak, for the World of Speech is the World of Fear. But when you speak about matters of love and fear, you should first feel fear, then fiery enthusiasm.

*Tzava'as HaRivash, p. 10b*

∞

6-11 Before you speak, realize that the World of Speech – the Shechinah – is speaking through you.

**THERE** is no speech without thought, for a person first thinks about what he is going to say. Now, when you think before you speak, you will certainly be afraid and ashamed when you realize that the World of Speech – the Shechinah[1] – is speaking through you. Since the Shechinah incorporates all the Attributes such as fear, love, and beauty, you will fear the words themselves. For how can a person not be awed and ashamed when they know that they elicit the Shechinah and all Her Attributes? This is the meaning of: "They do His word" (Psalms 103:20); that is, they turn their speech into action.[2]

*Kesser Shem Tov, part 2, p. 5b*

∞

---

[1] The Shechinah – the Divine Presence – corresponds to the world of Malchut, which is the lowest Sefirah and incorporates in it all the upper Sefirot – the Divine Attributes.

[2] In Hebrew, the words "to do" and "to make" are the same – *asseh.*

6-12 A person is only considered to be a servant of G•d out of fear and love.

**SOME** people are depressed when they pray because they have an excess of melancholy.[1] Yet they imagine that they are praying with great fear of G•d. Others think that are praying out of great love for G•d, though it really due to red bile. However, when [a person prays] out of love of G•d, and suddenly feels ashamed when they long to glorify G•d and overcome their own evil inclination for His sake, then it is good.

For a person is not considered to be a servant of G•d unless it is out of fear and love. But this fear must come upon them suddenly, and not through their own efforts, which is the case of uplifting of the "Feminine waters." True fear, however, falls upon a person [suddenly], so that they forget where they are, their mind becomes purified, and their tears flow by themselves. If it is unlike this, though they may think that they love the Creator, their feelings are nothing. For this is the gate to G•d. Fear is the gate to love, and if they are not in the gate of fear, how can they be in love? A person like

---

[1] *Marah shechora*, literally, "black bile." This is based upon a medical theory that the body exudes various types of bile that effect the emotions. The point is that one may feel that they are praying with deveikut – spiritual attachment – whereas their emotions are merely a product of their physiology.

this isn't even a servant, and certainly not on a level for fear to descend upon them. They aren't doing the type of worship appropriate for a Jewish person at all. They merely serve G•d by rote. They think that they are serving Him in joy, but it is a corrupted form of happiness. Let them return to G•d with their whole heart and soul.

*Likutey Yikarim, p. 3*

∞

6-13 Speaking words of Torah and prayer with ulterior motives creates kelipot that enclothe themselves in wicked people who will take vengeance upon you.

"**WE** will make you circlets of gold with dots of silver." (Song of Songs 1:11) "Circlets of gold" is fear of G•d; "Dots of silver" means love of G•d.[1] That is, do not speak words of Torah and prayer with ulterior motives,[2] for that creates kelipot that enclothe themselves in wicked people who will take

---

[1] Kabbalistically, gold corresponds to the Sefirah of Gevurah, which is the root of fear of G•d. Silver, *kesef*, is related to the word "to long for" – *l'kesof* (לכסוף), implying love, and relates the Sefirah of Chesed.
[2] Such as to gain respect from others.

vengeance upon you. This is the meaning of [G•d's promise to Noah], that the wicked people of the generation would not kill him.[1] Understand this!

You also need more fear than love, the latter being called "dots of silver."

*Sefer Baal Shem Tov*

∞

---

[1] When he built the ark. See Rashi on Genesis 6:18.

CHAPTER 7

# CONCENTRATION
# IN PRAYER

## A. Total Concentration

7-a1 Praying with total concentration.

**THE** soul of the Baal Shem Tov told him, "You did not merit all these Supernal revelations because you learned Talmud and the legal codes but because you always pray with total concentration. This brought you to your high level."

*Tzava'as HaRivash 41*

∞

7-a2 Pray with single-minded concentration until you forget your physicality.

**YOU** should pray with total concentration, going from letter to letter until you forget your own physicality. Imagine that the letters are combining together, which generates great pleasure. This is the world of Yetzirah, the level of Daat. Next, you should ascend to the letters of thought until you no longer hear what you are saying. Then you come to the world of Beriyah, the level of Binah. Finally, you attain total nullification in which your entire physicality is annulled. This is the world of Atzilut,

the level of Chochmah.     Kesser Shem Tov, part 2
p. 17b

∞

7-a3 Be so devoid of physicality that no self-awareness or strength remains.

**AS** long as you can still intend to say, "Blessed are You," you have not reached the height of prayer. For you must be so devoid of physicality that not an ounce of self-awareness or strength remains in you.

*Avodas Yisroel, Metzorah*

∞

## B. Techniques

7-b1 Imagine that you are going to die in your prayers.

**IMAGINE** that you are going to die during your prayers because of your great concentration. Indeed, some people concentrate so intensely that in fact they should die after several words. When you recall this, ask yourself, "Why should I feel proud or self-conscious during this prayer since I'm willing to die after a few words?" In actuality, it is only because of G•d's great kindness that you have the ability to finish your prayers and remain alive.

*Tzava'as HaRivash 42*

∞

7-b2 G•d's keeps people alive after prayer.

**IT** is only G•d's great kindness that keeps people alive after prayer. For with all the energy and concentration that they put into their words, it would be natural for them to die of exhaustion.

*Tzava'as HaRivash 35*

7-b3 Remaining alive after prayer is a miracle.

**IT** is a veritable miracle that a person re-mains alive after prayer — that due to their intensely resolute attachment to G•d, their soul does not leave them.

*Sifsei Tzaddikim, Beshalach*

∞

7-b4 Asking for G•d's help and assistance.

**IT** is impossible to pray with concentration without receiving help. Ask G•d for His help and assistance.

*Tzava'as HaRivash 41*

∞

7-b5 In prayer, one must feel the surrounding light.

**IT** is impossible to pray properly unless you can feel the light fully surrounding and enveloping you from all sides.

*Likkutim Yikarim p. 2a*

7-b6 In your prayers, don't expend all your energy at the beginning.

**YOU** should go level by level in your prayers. Do not expend all your energy at the beginning. Rather, start slowly, and by the middle, you can attach yourself with great cleaving to G•d. Then, you will even be able to pray more quickly without a loss of intent.

Even though you may not pray with mystical attachment from the beginning, you should still say the words with great concentration. Keep applying yourself until G•d helps you pray with great attachment.

*Tzava'as HaRivash 32*

∞

7-b7 Say prayers with all of your strength.

**SIMILARLY**, there is "a flaming sword that revolves to guard the path of the Tree of Life."[1] When you wish to attach your thoughts to the Creator during prayer, the kelipot will not let you. Nevertheless, in spite of this obstacle, you must force yourself with all your strength during prayer,

---

[1] Genesis 3:24

to attach yourself to Him. Then you will enter the Supernal worlds.

Strengthen yourself in believing with perfect faith that "the whole world is full of His glory"[1] and this will lead you to the Supernal worlds. Thus it is written, "The righteous live by their faith."[2]

Likewise, if your attachment wanes in the middle of prayer, say the words of prayer with as much concentration as you can gather. Make a full, all-embracing effort to regain your previous level, even if it takes many attempts.

At first, you should cling to the form of the word,[3] and then, give the word its soul.[4] Start by infusing all of your physical strength as you say the words until the power of your soul will shine within you. As the Zohar states, "If wood does not burn, splinter it."[5] In time, you will be able to serve G•d in your thoughts alone, without any movements of your body.

*Tzava'as HaRivash 58*

---

[1] Isaiah 6:3
[2] Habakkuk 2:4
[3] Literally translated from the original as the "body" of the word, this refers to its basic meaning.
[4] This refers to the deeper meaning found in the liturgy that is available once one's soul is invested in the words and divested from physicality.
[5] Zohar 3:168a

7-b8 Pray in a low voice and say the words with all of your strength.

**TRAIN** yourself to pray in a low voice, even Pesukei D'Zimrah.[1] Though you scream out inside of yourself, speak the words of prayer in a whisper. In fact, say the words with all of your strength whether during your prayers or your Torah study. As it is written, "All my bones will say, G•d, who is like You!"[2] That is, this crying out, born out of attachment to G•d, should be in a whisper.

*Tzava'as HaRivash 33*

∞

7-b9 Concentrate fully on saying the words of Torah until you see the gleaming lights innately residing within the words.

**CONCENTRATE** fully on the words of prayer and Torah that you are saying, until you see the lights within the words which illuminate each other and the numerous lights emerging from within them all. As is said, "Light is sown for the right-

---

[1] (lit. verses of praise); The selection of passages which appear early in the morning prayer service and lead into the declaration of faith.
[2] Psalms 35:10

eous, and joy for the upright in heart."[1] The letters of Torah are G•d's chambers into which He shines the emanation of His light, as the Zohar states, "The Holy One and the Torah are One."[2]

Put all your intention – your soul – into the words of Torah. The conscious intention which you develop and subsequently possess can only be found in the soul. Known as deveikut, this is full divestment of physicality. When you strip your soul of your body, so that your soul clothes itself in the thoughts that you speak, you will see many Supernal worlds. "The Holy One, the Torah and Israel are all One."

*Kesser Shem Tov, part 2 p. 4d*

∞

## C. Small-mindedness

7-c1 At least pray with a little bit of concentration.

**BE** content if G•d helps you concentrate fully for half of the prayers or even most of them. If your attachment to G•d falters or disappears, pray as

---

[1] Psalms 97:11
[2] Zohar 2:85b, 3:73a

best as you can even though it is done with less
concentration.

*Tzava'as HaRivash p.7a*

∞

7-c2 Serving G•d with constricted consciousness.

**SOMETIMES**, a person can only serve G•d
with mochin d'katnus.[1] They do not enter the
Supernal worlds at all but merely think about how
the whole world is filled with His glory and that G•d
is close to them. At that point, they are like a child
whose mind has only partially developed. Nonethe-
less, though they serve G•d in this way, it is done
with great spiritual attachment.

*Tzava'as HaRivash 67*

∞

---

[1] Literally meaning small-mindedness, this term refers to a
constricted consciousness or perception.

7-c3 Even with limited thoughts cleave to G•d when you fall from your spiritual level.

**EVEN** when you fall from a loftier spiritual level, you should continue cleaving to G•d albeit with more limited thoughts. Even with this impediment, you can still reach an intense spiritual level for as long as one spark remains in a coal, it can be fanned into a great fire. But if even this small spark is missing, it cannot be stoked. So too, if a person does not constantly cleave to G•d by whatever means possible, their soul can be completely extinguished, G•d forbid.

*Likkutei Yikarim p.15b*

∞

7-c4 A person is where his thoughts are.

**EVEN** when you are in a state of limitation, you can still maintain a great attachment to the Shechinah for when you think about the Supernal worlds, you will be there. A person is where his thoughts are, and if they were not in the Supernal worlds, they would not be able to think of them.

*Tzava'as HaRivash 69*

7-c5 When you cannot pray, concentrate and draw fear upon yourself.

**WHEN** you cannot pray, don't assume that you won't be able to for the rest of the day. Rather, push yourself, and draw more fear upon yourself. Be like a king who disguises himself and goes out to war. The intelligent people will recognize the king by his mannerisms, while those who are not as smart can still discern his majesty through other signs for the king is found wherever there is great joy.

Likewise, when you cannot pray with concentration, realize that the guards surround the King. The King is really there, only you cannot approach due to all the protection surrounding Him. You must push yourself to feel fear, so that you can approach and pray to Him. Then you will be able to pray with great concentration.

*Tzava'as HaRivash 72*

∞

7-c6 Concentration on prayers during the week.

**DON'T** think, "On Shabbat, I will concentrate on my prayers but not during the week." This is not the way of a faithful servant, but rather one who serves the king only when he is present.[1] Rather, tell the King how dreadful life is without Him. Push past all the guards until you stand before the King Himself. Even if you cannot say a word and are unfit to be there, the King will fulfill your requests for His compassion upon you is very great.

*Tzava'as HaRivash 85*

∞

7-c7 Weakening the body and mind through prayers.

**EVEN** though on Shabbat and Festivals you pray the morning and musaf[2] prayers with deveikut, if need be, you can pray the afternoon prayer with less deveikut for your body and mind have been weakened from the morning prayers.

*Likkutim Yikarim p. 2c*

---

[1] Shabbat, being a day totally devoted to G•d, represents an increase in His presence.
[2] An additional prayer service recited on Shabbat and Festivals commemorating the additional offerings brought in the Temple on these days.

7-c8 Without fear and love, prayers and studies do not ascend.

**IT** is written, "All the days of the poor are evil."[1] Our Rabbis have stated, "The only poverty is the lack of knowledge."[2] Thus, "All the days of the poor" – in knowledge – "are bad." Their prayers and studies are worthless to G•d for they lack fear and love and do not ascend.

"But the Talmud asks, "what about Shabbat and Festivals?"[3] Certainly, then, everyone receives inspiration from above and prays with greater concentration. The Talmud answers, "A change in routine is the beginning of illness." And even though they pray with greater intensity, this only makes them proud, and they imagine that they have attained a high level. Thus even then, his days are bad. Therefore, their evil inclination is aroused by eating and drinking.[4] Therefore, their evil inclination is aroused because "a change in routine is the beginning of illness."

*Tzava'as HaRivash 131*

---

[1] Proverbs 15:15
[2] Talmud *Nedarim* 41a
[3] Bava Basra 146a
[4] Zohar I:110a

7-c9 Addressing G•d.

**WE** pray, "You are He, our G•d."[1] At first, one addresses G•d directly – "You" – and then indirectly – "He". If you think that you are attached to G•d and that you stand before Him, then, to the contrary, you are really distant. But, if you realize that you are far, then you are close. Thus, the one who thinks "You" is really on the level of "He," but when one thinks "He," then He is "our G•d"[2].

*Toldos Yaakov Yosef, Kedoshim*

∞

## D. The Fruit of Concentration

7-d1 The prayer-leader and the congregation must understand their respective responsibility.

**THE** congregation errs when they draw out their prayers and prevent the chazan[3] from concluding each section of the liturgy. They prevent him from bestowing blessings on them[4] for in

---

[1] From the end of the morning prayers
[2] An even more distant reference
[3] (lit. cantor); One who leads the congregation in prayer.
[4] The chazan acts as a channel for drawing blessing through the Shechinah, which then passes to the entire congregation.

waiting for them to finish, his concentration is weakened. The congregation must be very cautious of this for they stand to lose much goodness. Indeed, great and serious effort is required by the chazan and congregation in order to know how to act during prayer. But the chazan bears the greater responsibility.

Ohr HaMeir, Tetzaveh

∞

7-d2 All the mystical intentions are included in words recited with great passion.

**WHEN** you pray with mystical intentions, you can only use those intentions that you know. But when you recite each word with great passion, all the mystical intentions which you possess are included in your words. In every letter resides a complete world, and when you say the words with great emotion, you arouse those worlds above. Therefore, you should pray with great attachment and fervor, which will unquestionably have an effect in the upper worlds. This is because every letter makes its mark above.

Tzava'as HaRivash 118

7-d3 Understanding the simple meaning of the words of prayer.

**WHETHER** in Torah study or in prayer, if you understand the simple meaning of the words or the practical law to be derived from your studies, you bind Malchut to Binah.

*Toldos Yaakov Yosef, Va'eschanan*

∞

7-d4 The practice of praying with mystical intentions.

**A** hungry person wants to eat something tasty and sees some food on some high place beyond his reach. He can imagine that he is eating it, but does that really help? In fact, the more he thinks about the food, the hungrier he gets. So too, people who practice thinking lofty and awesome mystical intentions which stand at the height of the Creation, yet their minds cannot grasp them for they are unable to perform mystical intentions. How, then, does their practice help? It would be better if they did not try to reach this high place – that so transcends their level and comprehension.

*Ohr HaMeir, Vayeirah*

# CHAPTER 8

# CONSTRICTED CONSCIOUSNESS

8-1 A person cannot pray with enthusiasm because their limbs feel heavy.

**SOMETIMES**, a person longs to pray with enthusiasm but cannot because their limbs feel heavy. Thus King David prayed, "Do not cast me off in the time of old age"[1] – when my limbs feel heavy like those of an old person.

*Ohr Torah, Eikev*

∞

8-2 With the passing of time, a person's service of G•d can fall into old age.

**THE** verse states, "Do not cast me off in the time of old age[2]" for it can happen that with the passing of time, a person's service of G•d falls into old age.

*Ohr HaMeir, Yisro*

∞

---

[1] Psalms 71:9
[2] Psalms 71:9

8-3 A person can become excited to serve G•d through Torah study or prayer, but their desire becomes immediately lost.

**SOMETIMES**, a person becomes excited to serve G•d through Torah study or prayer, but their desire does not age slowly. Rather, it becomes immediately lost as though the mitzvah had become old. This is similar to, ". . . like an old decree."[1] Thus it says, "Do not cast me off" from my enthusiasm that my worship should seem to be like an old decree. Rather, let it be like a new edict from the King.

*Sifsei Tzaddikim, Pikudei*

∞

8-4 G•d pushes a person away in order to draw them nearer.

**IF** a tzaddik finds that he is losing time from his Torah study or prayer, he should regard this as if G•d is pushing him away in order to draw them

---

[1] One should recite the *Shema* with fear and trembling, like a newly issued decree and not like an old edict that no longer inspires fear.

closer. This is the meaning of, "His left hand is under my head, and his right hand embraces me."[1]

*Toldos Yaakov Yosef, Vayeishev*

∞

8-5 Praying with constricted consciousness.

**SOMETIMES** you pray with constricted consciousness, and suddenly in one minute, the light of your soul shines and rises to the Supernal.[2] This is like a person who climbs a ladder. Thus it is written, "Send Your light and Your truth, they will lead me"[3].

*Likkutei Yikarim p.3d*

---

[1] Song of Songs 2:6
[2] The *Degel Machane Ephraim* writes a similar thought: "A song of ascents, I lift my eyes to the mountains, from where will my help come?" (Psalms 121:1) "I lift my eyes to the mountains" – to the higher levels of consciousness for the "mountains" are the "Forefathers." When I see that at times this consciousness leaves me, G•d forbid, then "from where (*m'ayin*) will my help come?" Because I see and understand this, my heart is broken and I become nothing (*ayin*). Therefore, my help will come from the Infinite (*Ein Sof*)." The meaning of this passage is that when a person, having lost the connection with G•d, becomes humble and contrite and makes himself like nothing (*ayin),* then a new light shines on him from a light whose source is the One Without End.
[3] Psalms 43:3

CHAPTER 9

# EXTRANEOUS THOUGHTS

## A. Nature of extraneous thoughts

9-a1 Foreign thoughts are like revelations that a person has in their dreams.

**A** person must be exceedingly clever in dealing with foreign thoughts that come to him during prayer, for they are his very own powers that come to him to be fixed. These foreign or extraneous thoughts are like revelations that a person has in his dreams, where the matter is not explicitly revealed but is clothed and hidden within some act which represents the thoughts. Thus, a person must be very wise to appreciate the implications of the dream (and the extraneous thoughts) in order to understand and fix the underlying matter by way of removing the limitations relating to this matter(s). Once he fixes the underlying matter, he will begin to pray with even greater intensity and spiritual attachment. Through this, he uplifts the sparks of holiness.

*Divrei Moshe, Lech Lecha*

∞

9-a2 Uplifting of the sparks is done through the extraneous thoughts that enter the mind during prayer.

**EVERY** day, your prayers require a different intention – "if he is able to say something new."[1] Proof for this lies in the essence of prayer, which is to redeem the 288 sparks from the broken vessels. This is the meaning of "uplifting the feminine waters" to Malchut, which causes the two halves to unite.[2]

Elevating these sparks comes through the extraneous thoughts that enter the mind during prayer. A wise person knows how to extract the essence of these thoughts, which are the sparks of holiness within the impure shell that forms the thought itself.[3] For instance, lustful thoughts, which come from Chesed (as it is written, "If a man takes his sister[4] . . . it is chesed"[5]) at their essential

---

[1] Talmud B*crachos* 29b
[2] This refers to the essential unification of G•d.
[3] A person should not be so foolish as to engage in "sublimation of the midot" of extraneous thought for such things were intended only for Tzaddikim Tanya ch. 28.
[4] Leviticus 20:17
[5] According to most Biblical commentators, *chesed* in Aramaic means "shameful." The Baal Shem Tov, however, follows the Hebrew meaning of the word, which is "love" or "kindness." The underlying idea is that all desire, even the most illicit, has a root in holiness. However, that emotion fell to an impure,

root. You should realize that the pleasure in these thoughts only exists because of the single spark of holiness within it. How much greater, then, is the pleasure of clinging to its root?

On two consecutive day's, can it be said that one's thoughts are ever alike? Necessarily, then, the prayers one recites based on these ever changing thoughts must also be different. But it requires profound insight and intense concentration to align one's heart, mouth and thoughts. To be sure, this is not the case if you pray by rote as you did yesterday and on other previous days. Your tongue just reels off the words, and your head bows by itself at the appropriate time, but your heart is missing.

For this reason, there are ten terms for prayer, which correspond to the ten attributes in Malchut. Each day, you must repair another spark of the ten aspects of Malchut, until you fix the last aspect and return in repentance. This is especially relevant for the generation before Moshiach, when the entire world will be rectified down to the "heels" at which time all the sparks of the universe will

---

material state. The task of man, therefore, is to uplift all thoughts and emotions to their Supernal root.

ascend. Then, "death will be swallowed up forever,"[1] and Moshiach will come.

According to this, you should remember that your prayers are not for yourself but for the sake of the Shechinah. As the Arizal writes, "If you think about your own needs, the Shechinah cries out over you, 'G•d has delivered me into their hands; I am unable to rise.'[2] But if your intention is for the good of the Shechinah, you will be answered immediately for 'If the Shechinah is there, they [the Supernal gates] immediately open for the supplicant.'[3] Furthermore, your request is included in Binah, which is the "mother of all life." And since all souls are included in the Shechinah, you will be answered, as well. On the other hand, if you pray for the Shechinah in order to be answered, you make a partition ... a wall, for all intents and purposes. May G•d enlighten us to serve him in truth and simplicity!"

The sign that your prayers will be answered is alluded to in the verse, "You will direct their heart, Your ear will hear."[4] If G•d helps you concentrate on your prayers, then certainly "Your ear will hear." Were it not an opportune time to

[1] Isaiah 25:8
[2] Lamentations 1:14
[3] Tikkunei Zohar p. 55a
[4] Psalms 10:17

enter the King's chamber and receive an answer, you would be unable to concentrate. But since you have entered before the King, your request will surely be granted for nothing can prevent G•d from fulfilling your desires and heartfelt requests for He is the ultimate love and compassion.

Yet, there are times when you come before the King, but your request goes unanswered. This can be understood with the parable of the king whose consort has sinned. The king dismisses her, and she travels to a distant land. One day, the king must go there on royal affairs. When his consort hears that he is coming, she devises a plan to see him. She comes before him and pleads with him. She tells him how bitter her life has been since she left him, and she relates to him everything that happened to her since. Then, the king forgives her and fulfills her requests. However, if she approaches him with threats and accusations, claiming that he betrayed her, he will not listen unless she finds him in good spirits. Then her words will make an impression on him, and he will realize that her claim of abandonment was correct and that his actions were unfitting for a king. Then he will fulfill her request and answer her favorably, despite the fact that she spoke harshly. This is known as the "Shechinah quarreling with her husband."

*Toldos Yaakov Yosef p. 181a*

∞

9-a3 When you pray, the Divine Presence clothes itself in you and speaks your words.

**AS** soon as you pray, "L•rd, open my lips...,"[1] the Divine Presence clothes itself in you and speaks your words. If you believe this, you will be fearful and awestruck for G•d reduces Himself, as it were, to dwell within you. As it says, "He peers through the cracks"[2] — through the letters, which are themselves palaces. During prayer, you go from one palace to another, and you are continually judged if you are worthy to enter. This judgment occurs when the extraneous thoughts enter your mind. If you only realized this, you would pray with greater concentration. The problem is that you forget that they are judging you.

*Likkutei Amarim p. 1b*

---

[1] Psalms 51:17. This verse is recited at the beginning of the *Amidah*. The implication is that the mouth declares G•d's own words of praise, not merely our praise of Him.
[2] Song of Songs 2:9

9-a4 When the impure shells hear the voice of one's prayer, they try and interrupt the person's prayers with foreign and empty thoughts.

**WHEN** the Jewish people pray and attach themselves to G•d, a voice calls out, "Go out and see, O' Daughters of Zion."[1] If you are not ready or able to make this union, they tell you to "go out," but if you are ready, you will "see."[2]

When the impure shells hear this voice, they try to interrupt a person's prayers with foreign and empty thoughts. But a smart person will cling to their Creator in love and fear. This uplifts the sparks of life within these thoughts. Ask yourself, "Why should I cling to the material aspect of the things when it is better to cling to its inner essence, which derives from G•d's Chochmah? Is it not written, 'You have made them all with wisdom?'"[3]

*Kesser Shem Tov, part 2 p. 19b*

∞

---

[1] Song of Songs 3:11
[2] Referring to spiritual perception
[3] Psalms 104:24

9-a5 When a person prays, they hurl distracting thoughts at him, and he is immediately outside the words.

**THE** Zohar explains that a person is judged in each palace and expelled if he is found unworthy.[1] The Baal Shem Tov taught that words of prayer are these very "palaces", for the intellect dwells within them. When a person prays, he goes from letter to letter and from word to word. If he is unworthy, distracting thoughts are hurled at him, and he is immediately thrown outside the palace.[2]

*Kesser Shem Tov, part 2 p. 7b*

∞

---

[1] Zohar 1:234a

[2] R. Menachem Mendel of Vitebsk writes that extraneous thoughts can only enter the mind of a person who is unhappy with his level of worship. He compares this to a peasant who tries to enter the palace of the king. Since he does not belong there, the guards push him out. So too, a person who tries to pray and serve G•d on a higher level than is appropriate for them will be pushed away by foreign thoughts. However, a person who is happy with his level, even if it is not very high, will be able to pray with clarity. Since they are in their place, nothing can push them out.

9-a6   You should be ashamed about the foreign thought you have while praying.

**YOU** should be ashamed of the foreign thought you have while praying. Understand that you are being expelled from the King's palace. You should return in shame and submission. Harboring foreign thoughts is tantamount to giving birth to an illegitimate child as the Talmud states, "one sheep follows the other."[1]

Thought has a masculine and feminine aspect; and voice and speech are masculine and feminine.[2] If you concentrate on a foreign thought while speaking holy words, the words are like an illegitimate child whose body is normal but whose soul is tainted.[3] Here, the words are formed from holy letters, while the thought behind them is bad. Because with holy speech joined to thoughts of something else, you create a mamzer.

Also remember, that while your thought is wandering among other matters, the Holy One, blessed be He, says "Why did you come into the

[1] Talmud *Kesuvos* 103a
[2] Voice is non-differentiated sound and is considered masculine. Speech gives shape and meaning to sound and is considered feminine. This follows the principle that the vessel – the feminine aspect – gives form to the expansive masculine element.
[3] The Sages consider the soul of an illegitimately conceived individual to be blemished by the sinful act of his parents.

tevah (word) while there is no man (man's thoughts, which are the very soul of his speech) in the words.

*Tzava'as HaRivash 89*

∞

9-a7 When a soul ascends, it is tested in each world to see if it is worthy to enter.

**A** human being is composed of numerous forces, each one necessary for another Supernal world. When their soul ascends, it is tested in each world to see if it is worthy to enter. If not, it is pushed out. Sometimes, the forces do this by sending extraneous thoughts. However, if the person is smart, through that very thought, he can cling to G•d even more. The thought is composed of letters, which are the "limbs" of the Divine Presence. These letters fell among the "shells" due to the primordial "Breaking of the Vessels," causing them to become arranged in evil patterns. This is like serving delicacies that are all intermingled. Although each one alone is good, when combined, they are distasteful. So too, these letters have become bad.

But when a person understands the true nature of the thought — for instance, desirous thoughts have fallen from the realm of desire,[1] fearful thoughts from the realm of fear,[2] prideful thoughts from Tiferes – and directs them to G•d, the person returns them to their source. The same is true of the other attributes, for each thought reflects a different Supernal attribute from which it fell. When a person attaches an extraneous thought to its respective attribute, the shell falls away and it forms a good letter combination as it is said, "They open the cords and the sacks fall."[3]

G•d has great delight in this like a king's son who has fallen into captivity. When he is returned back to the king, his father the king is much happier than if his son had been with him the whole time.

*Kesser Shem Tov, part 2 p. 3a*

∞

---

[1] Related to *Chesed*
[2] Related to *Gevurah*
[3] Talmud *Shabbat* 153a

9-a8 When foreign thoughts enter your mind, you should realize that there are Judgments upon you that want to harm you.

**WHEN** sinful thoughts enter your mind, you should realize that there are judgments against you that want to harm you. In such a case, you should be extremely concerned and make a unification between "fear" and "awe." Then "all the workers of iniquity will disband."[1]

The verses state, "And it came to pass, when Abraham approached to Egypt, that he said to Sarai his wife, 'I know now that you are an attractive woman.'"[2] And "When the local men asked Isaac about his wife, he said, 'She is my sister' for he was afraid 'lest the men of the place should kill me for Rebecca because she is fair to look upon.'"[3] The fact that he started thinking about her beauty was a sign of impending disaster.[4]

*Katones Pasim p. 42d*

---

[1] Psalms 92:10
[2] Genesis 12:11
[3] Genesis 26:7
[4] The Sages explain that before these occasions, neither Abraham nor Isaac recognized their wives' beauty. According to the Baal Shem Tov, the fact that these *tzaddikim* suddenly became attracted to physical beauty was a sign that there were Supernal Judgments upon them, as reflected in the Egyptians and Philistines who threatened to kill them.

9-a9 The impure shells ride on the words of your prayer.

**IF** you have foreign thoughts when you pray, G•d forbid, the kelipot ride on your words as thought rides upon the words of speech. This is the meaning of the verse, "to the horses of the chariot of Pharaoh, I have compared you, my beloved."[1] Words of speech are called "horses." When Pharaoh – the foreign thought – rides upon them, then "I have compared you (dimisicha), my beloved" – it would be better to be silent.[2] However, "a word that comes from the heart, enters the heart," i.e., they enter the heart of Above, by means of the breaten, as it is well known.

*Tzava'as HaRivash 71*

∞

---

[1] Song of Songs 1:9
[2] The etymological root of *dimisicha* is *domeh*, which is related to the word *dumiah* meaning "silence." Thus, at a time when foreign thoughts ride on one's words of prayer, it would be better to be silent.

## B. When the mind cannot concentrate

9-b1 Be quick and careful to avoid having foreign thoughts during prayer.

**PEOPLE** must be quick and careful to avoid having foreign thoughts during prayer. There was a very dangerous road that passed through a forest filled with bandits and marauders who would beat and rob those who passed through. A person had to race through this forest at top speed to survive. Once, two men traveled through this forest. One was dead drunk, while the other was sober. The sober man went quickly, until he came out safely from the other side. The drunk, however, treaded on step-by-step. The robbers caught and beat him, yet he didn't feel anything.

When the two friends met later, the first one couldn't believe what happened to the second. "How did you survive all those terrible blows?" he asked. The drunk, however, was equally amazed, for he hadn't been aware of anything that happened to him. He thought that he had passed through the forest without incident. Finally, his friend showed him his wounds and blood-stained clothing in a mirror. He was still amazed, though, since he didn't remember anything.

The meaning of the parable is self-evident.
Divrei Moshe, Bo

∞

9-b2 If you're unable to concentrate because of extraneous thoughts, pray like a little child from the printed text.

**A** wise person knows when it is right to pray with the inner mystical intentions and to delight in mystical rapture. If, however, you are in a state of constrained consciousness and unable to concentrate because of being overwhelmed by extraneous thoughts, you should pray like a little child from the printed text. The Baal Shem Tov said that he was once in a foreign country for a period of time in this state of mind[1] for his expanded consciousness had left him. He therefore attached himself to the letters.

*Katones Pasim, Balak*

---

[1] This happened in Istanbul during the Baal Shem Tov's attempted journey to the Land of Israel.

9-b3 When you are on a low level, pray from a prayer book.

**WHEN** you are on a low level, pray from a prayer book because seeing the letters will help you concentrate. However, when you cleave to the Upper Worlds, it is better for you to close yours eyes so as not to see anything that might interrupt your dveikut.

*Tzava'as HaRivash 40*

∞

9-b4 Do not mock a person who gesticulates during prayer.

**A** person drowning in a river makes all sorts of strange gestures to save themselves. No one would mock them for doing so. So too, a person who gesticulates during prayer.[1] Do not mock them for they arc saving themselves from the "evil waters,"[2] which seek to disrupt their thoughts and prayers.

*Likkutim Yikarim p. 15a*

---

[1] Early chassidim were known to move wildly during their prayers, at times even performing somersaults.
[2] Psalms 124:5

9-b5 You should recite *Keriyat Shema¹* twice a day without having distracting thoughts.

**YOU** should, at the very least, recite Shema twice a day without having distracting thoughts. The effect of this is great beyond measure. One who recites Shema distances him from all harms in the world, whether they relate to the body or the soul. And though it is impossible to pray without having any foreign thoughts, you should train yourself to avoid them at the beginning of reading the Shema.

*Tzava'as HaRivash 19*

∞

9-b6 Ulterior motives in serving G•d will create an actual person.

**ULTERIOR** motives in serving G•d are a complete structure² and will create an actual person who will torment you.

*Tzafnah Paneach p. 18a*

---

¹ Reading Shema
² Implying that ulterior motives have all the elements of a body – head, body, and limbs.

## C. What foreign thoughts teach you

9-c1 Experiencing foreign and confusing thoughts during prayer is a good sign.

**THE** fact that a person experiences foreign and confusing thoughts during prayer is actually a good sign. We can explain this by way of a parable. A king in his palace is surrounded by many walls and guards to keep people away. If a person wants to make a request of the king but the guards sense that it will be bad for them, they will not let him enter. However, if they think that he is an unimportant person and that the king will not fulfill his request, they let him through. What difference does it make to them? However, they will do all that they can to prevent an important minister to enter since they know that the king will listen to him, and it will be bad for them.[1]

The same applies to prayer, which is attachment to G•d in order to redeem the Holy Sparks from the side of evil and lowly things. This is also

---

[1] In this case, the gate-keepers represent the forces of illusion that keep people from recognizing and drawing close to G•d. These manifest themselves in the consciousness as the distracting thoughts and desires that arise during prayer. These forces (and thoughts) are only enlivened by a spark of holiness that is exiled within them. The *tzaddik* wants to redeem this spark and bring it to the King, thereby robbing them of their power and negating them. Thus, they opposed his entry into the palace.

bad for them. But if a simple person, whose prayers are not so good and who makes little impression, approaches G•d – the king's guard ignore him and do not confuse him too much. This is not the case with a G•d-fearing person whose prayers bear fruit below and in their supernal root above. The side of evil does everything it can to disturb him with foreign thoughts. If the person is smart enough to realize this, they will fight with all their might and cry out bitterly, "Father, save me!" Then, the Holy One, Who longs for the prayers of Israel, will open all the doors for them and bring about a rectification, uplifting the Holy Sparks and bring the Redemption.

*Sefas Emes, Va'eirah*

∞

9-c2 Force yourself to pray at those times when you think you cannot.

**DO** not tell yourself, "I pray enthusiastically when I can, but otherwise, I will not force myself" – for the opposite should apply. When a king comes to the battlefield, he disguises himself so that the enemy will not recognize him and try to kill him.

Yet, his servants nearby can discern him from his mannerisms, and those who are far off can tell that the troops are guarding a certain place. The king is probably there.

This also applies to prayer. The distracting thoughts and emotions are guarding the King so that you cannot see Him. You should therefore push yourself even more, for the King is there. They are merely hiding Him from you.

*Tzava'as HaRivash 85*

∞

9-c3 Realize that G•d is there even when He pushes you away.

**EVEN** though Rabbi Nechunia ben HaKaneh knew all the mystical intentions of prayer, he still prayed with the simplicity of a small child. This is because there are two aspects of serving G•d – one on His left side when G•d pushes a person away, and the other on His right when He draws a person closer. This is reflected in the statement, "When you refer to G•d by the Name 'Ado-nai,' remember that He is L•rd over everything. At the same time, keep in mind the written meaning of the Tetragramma-

135

ton — that G•d "is, was and will be," and that He brings all the worlds into existence."[1]

Thus, when you say the words "Blessed are You," realize that G•d stands right before you and that He "is, was and will be." There is no greater pleasure for G•d than your mentioning His Name and speaking to Him face to face, as it is written, "Let him kiss me with the kisses of his mouth"[2] and "His right hand will embrace me."[3] On the other hand, if your sins distance you from G•d so that when you say, "Blessed are You," your mind is flooded with mundane thoughts, you cannot concentrate and you lose the wondrous pleasure of "the kisses of his mouth." This is the "left hand" of the Holy One.

Nevertheless, even when His left hand completely rejects you, it is only so that His right hand will receive you in repentance. A smart person will realize that G•d is there even when He pushes him away. In order for one person to push another, one must be right there – right in front of him. Therefore, he will accept His rejection in love, kiss it and be in great fear, knowing that it is meant to bring him even closer. For His right hand is outstretched to embrace the penitent.

---

[1] Tur Orach Chayim Sec. 5
[2] Song of Songs 1:2
[3] Song of Songs 2:6

So too, one should use the experience of externally generated fears to come to an inner fear of G•d. There is inner goodness of the bad thoughts themselves even though G•d's kisses are surely better than His rebuffs.

*Katones Pasim p. 43b*

∞

## D. Repairing and redeeming the words of foreign thoughts

9-d1 Rearranging the letters or words of foreign thoughts in prayer.

**WHEN** you have foreign thoughts in prayer, think of how everything comes from the letters making up the thoughts. These letters are holy, and it is only your mind that has combined them into foolish patterns. If you can rearrange these letters to spell out holy words, it is very good. Alternatively, you can rearrange the words of the foreign thoughts, or divide one word into two, or extract the first letters of the words, just as long as you do not lose your spiritual attachment.

*Darchei Tzedek 25*

9-d2 You must fix the sparks that belong to you.

**WHOEVER** says *"Shema, Shema . . ."* [1] — Foreign thoughts that come to you during prayer or learning Torah contain those very sparks of holiness that you yourself caused to fall, whether in your present incarnation, a previous one or from the sin of Adam who contained all the souls of Israel. Thus, each Jew must fix the sparks that belong to him, for when you pray and long to attach yourself to holiness, those sparks also come to be repaired. One must be very insightful[2] about foreign thoughts during prayer for they are one's own strengths that come to be repaired.

*Divrei Moshe, Lech Lecha*

∞

---

[1] That is, if he recites the prayer *Keriyat Shema* twice in a row.
[2] To be able to discern the point of holiness that the thought contains.

9-d3 Negative and foreign thoughts enter a person's mind during prayer in order to be fixed and uplifted.

**"IF** a person says 'Shema, Shema' [1] we silence him.

But perhaps he wasn't concentrating the first time?

So what? Is he G•d's friend?[2] If he doesn't concentrate the first time, we hit him with a hammer until he does."[3]

The question still remains, however. Maybe he didn't concentrate the first time and now he is trying to concentrate so as to fulfill his obligation. Also, why is the example of the Shema chosen as opposed to something else?

The answer lies in the meaning of "accepting the yoke of heaven." A person must believe that the entire world is filled with G•d's glory and that is no place devoid of Him. G•d exists in all of a person's thoughts, and each one of them is a complete structure. Negative and foreign thoughts enter a person's mind during prayer in order to be fixed and uplifted. One must know with full clarity that a

---

[1] That is, if he recites the first word of the *Shema* twice in a row.
[2] That he can be so casual to recite the words of *Shema* without concentration.
[3] Talmud *Berachos* 33b

person who does not believe this, has not fully accepted the yoke of heaven. In fact, they are setting limitations to G•d's being which is a sharp contradiction to the belief that G•d exists in all of a person's thoughts.

Why would a person say "Shema, Shema?" Probably because he was not concentrating the first time, for he had foreign thoughts. Yet, had he realized that G•d's Presence is in that thought as well, he would not have had to say it twice.

This is expressed in the Talmud's terse language, "We hit him with a hammer" – his own thoughts strike him like a hammer in order to be fixed and uplifted. Saying Shema twice, on the other hand, suggests that G•d wasn't there the first time. This person limits G•d's existence and his own acceptance of the yoke of heaven. Thus, we silence him.

This explains the Talmud's statement, "If a chick dies in its shell, from where does its spirit leave? In the same way that it came in."[1] For it is taught, "If you see eggs in a dream, your supplications are being held in abeyance. If you see broken ones, your supplications are answered."[2] Eggs corresponds to prayer. Every thought is a complete

---

[1] Talmud *Bechoros* 8b
[2] Talmud *Berachos* 57a. Just as the insides of an egg are revealed (Rashi, loc. cit.)

entity; even an evil or foreign thought comes to you to be repaired and uplifted. If you reject that thought, you have rejected and killed a complete entity.

Yet sometimes, certain thoughts must be pushed away. How do you differentiate between them and the ones that should be drawn close and uplifted? Think about what happened when the thought came to your mind. If you immediately understood how to rectify and elevate it, then draw it close to you and do so. But if you did not immediately realize how to fix it, then it is most likely coming to disturb you and take your mind off of your prayers. Then, you can push it away for "if a person comes to kill you, rise up and kill him first."[1]

This is the meaning of, "If a chick dies in its shell, from where does its spirit leave?" A foreign thought during prayer – "an egg" – that "dies" – that you reject and kill – "from where does its spirit leave?" How dare you reject and kill a complete entity? The answer is, "The same way it came in." Just as it came in to distract you and push you away from G•d, that's how it leaves. You are allowed to cast it out of your thoughts.

---

[1] Talmud *Sanhedrin* 72a

Someone once asked if it is allowed to repeat several words of prayer that are said without concentration. The Baal Shem Tov answered, "It is well known that G•d's existence is in everything. Even extraneous thoughts contain sparks of holiness. Therefore, if you say a few words of prayer without concentration because of extraneous thoughts, you should realize that the thoughts came to have their spark removed. If you repeat the word, you show that G•d was not there the first time, and you thus limit G•d's existence. You shouldn't say them twice. Instead, you should think about and concentrate on those words in your mind."

*Ben Poras Yosef p. 50b-c, 53d*

∞

9-d4 Break your foreign thoughts during prayer to attach yourself to G•d.

**YOU** should break your foreign thoughts during prayer or Torah study and attach yourself to G•d. This repairs the holy spark that is located in that thought.

This is like a person counting money whose son has been taken captive. The son comes to him and demands, "Look, you have the money. Ransom me from captivity."

*Likkutei Yikarim p. 15c*

∞

9-d5 The foreign thoughts during each day's prayers come to a person in order to be repaired and uplifted.

**THE** Arizal writes that until the coming of Moshiach, no two prayers will ever be the same. This is the meaning of, "If a person makes his prayers fixed, they are not a supplication."[1]

This can be demonstrated by observing the foreign thoughts one has during prayer. These derive from the Breaking of the Vessels and the 288 sparks that a person must extract each day.[2] They come to a person in order to be repaired and

---

[1] Talmud *Berachot* 18b
[2] In the primordial Shattering of the Vessels, 288 sparks of holiness fell into the lower worlds. Fragments of these sparks are uplifted each day through Torah study and service of G•d. When all of the sparks have been redeemed, the Messianic Era will arrive.

uplifted. Thus, the foreign thoughts of each day are different.

If a person has wanton thoughts, he should attach them to their root in Chesed, thereby uplifting them. This is the inner meaning of the verse, "If a man takes his sister...it is disgraceful (chesed)."[1] Similarly, idolatrous thoughts blemish the beauty of Israel.[2]

*Toldos Yaakov Yosef, Vayakhel*

∞

9-d6 The true desire of holy sparks that enter your mind as foreign thoughts during prayer is that you repair and redeem them from the depths of the impure shells.

**IF** you do not study Torah and pray with love and fear of G•d, your words will not ascend.[3] All the more so if you have foreign thoughts, which are called "invalid offerings" for they are given over to negative forces. When you repent, however, you

---

[1] Leviticus 20:17
[2] See Lamentation 2:1. This is a reference to *Tiferet*. Idolatry is a fallen manifestation of this attribute in that the idol becomes a focus of adoration.
[3] Tikkunei Zohar, p. 25b

uplift those holy sparks, and they enter your mind as foreign thoughts during prayer or study. These are your very sins that fight against you. Their true desire, however, is for you to repair and redeem them from the depths of impurity. You do this by trembling at the realization that they are your sins and realizing that you must regret them.

*Toldos Yaakov Yosef p. 158a*

∞

9-d7 Elevate your thoughts from below to above.

**YOU** must elevate your thoughts from below to above, in the mystery of the 248 sparks.[1] Extraneous thoughts are all in Malchut of Malchut,[2] and when one enters your mind, you should

---

[1] According to the Arizal, at the time of the primordial Breakage of the Vessels, the lights of the vessels ascended to their source, and only the vessels themselves broke. However, 248 sparks of light remained in the vessels to enliven them. It is the main task of human beings throughout history to redeem these sparks from the *kelipah nogah* into which they fell, thus bringing the world to perfection.

[2] Each of the Sefirot contains aspects of all the others. The lowest Sefirah is Malchut, and the lowest aspect of Malchut is "Malchut of Malchut." It is from this lowest level that all the disruptive and extraneous come.

be scared of it.¹ By means of this fear, you unite "fear" and "awe" and remove the holy spark from the impure shell, which is the foreign thought itself.

Now, the thoughts of Rabbi Bun were pure and clear, and he could not uplift them, until it occurred to him to count the bricks of his house, or the chicks [in the case of Shmuel].

Furthermore, each of these cases also needs to be understood.²

*Toldos Yaakov Yosef, p. 209a*

∞

9-d8 Your prayers have been accepted if you can pray without extraneous thoughts.

**THERE** is a sign by which you can know if your prayers have been accepted. If you can pray without extraneous thoughts, at the very least, or ideally, with fear and love according to your level, then you know that your prayers have been accepted. Thus it says, "You will direct their heart,

---

¹ For they are pushing you away from the King, as the Baal Shem Tov explained elsewhere.
² See R. Tzaddok HaKohen of Lublin, *Tzidkas HaTzaddik* 233. It is worth noting that the word "chicks" (as in Shmuel's prayers) is *ephroach* (אפרוח), which has the letters RPCh in its root, that may allude to the 248 (רפ"ח) sparks that fell.

You will cause Your ear to hear."[1] It follows that when a person prays, he can know if his words were accepted and that G•d has listened.

*Toldos Yaakov Yosef, Behaloscha*

∞

9-d9 Chochmah, the location of thought, is the aspect of Judgment.

**TO** purify your thoughts, concentrate on the name כוז"ו.[2] Our Teacher and Master M.P.[3] wrote that this name is in Chochmah, the location of

---

[1] Psalms 10:17

[2] This name is constructed from the four letters of the Hebrew alphabet that follow the letters of the Tetragrammaton: כ follows י, ו follows ה, etc.. Rabbi Yitzchok Isaac of Komarno writes that this alludes to the heavenly dew that will revive the dead in the World to Come, for the word "dew" – *tal* – has the numerical value of 39, as does this Name. Each day, as well, there is a personal aspect of the Resurrection of the Dead, when the sparks of the Fallen Kings are enlivened. This happens by concentrating on the names טפטפי"ה כוזו זין ואו כף ואו זין ואו. In the future, there will be a universal resurrection, through the influence of *Mocha Setimah* (the Concealed Mind), which is the Dew of Onyx Stone, that removes all impurity and enlivens all the souls and the Kings that died. (*Zohar Chai, Terumah* 176).

[3] This apparently refers to Rabbi Meir Popperas (1624-1662), author of the famous Kabbalistic work *Pri Etz Chayim*, based upon the writings of the Arizal.

147

thought, which is the aspect of Judgment.[1] When spelled out in full, as follows, כ"ף וא"ו ז"י וא"ו א"א,[2] it has the numerical value of טפטפי"ה, the Name of thought.

*Siddur Rabbi Shabsai*

∞

9-d10 The sweetening of the 320 and 280 Judgments.

**I** tremble to relate the awesome things I heard from the Baal Shem Tov about the sweetening of the 320 and 280 Judgments,[3] and the rectification of improper thoughts through the Name Sha•dai, and its transposition [into the Name] *Kehat*,[4] as well as the YKVK, in its transposition into the Name *Kuzu*.[5] However, I only wrote down the main points on a piece of paper.

*Toldos Yaakov Yosef, p. 41b*

---

[1] Din.
[2] These are written on the outer side of a mezuzah.
[3] ש"כ ופ"ר דינים.
[4] תהכ – these three letters follow the letters of the Name Sha•dai in the Hebrew alphabet.
[5] וכוז – these letters also follow the four letters of the Tetragrammaton.

148

# CHAPTER 10

# UPLIFTING SPARKS

10-1 When a person knows that G•d is in every action in the world, there is nothing he cannot bear.

"**OUR** oxen are bearing (alupheinu me-subalim), with no breach, and no bad tidings, and no outcry in our streets."[1] When a person knows that the Master of the World (Alupho shel Olam) is in every action in the world, there is nothing he cannot bear. Then there is "no breach and no bad tidings."

The Baal Shem Tov taught, when you know that G•d's glory fills the whole world and that every action and thought comes from Him despite the fact that the language of certain prayers seems to contradict this, then "all the workers of iniquity will be disbanded"[2] – that is, all the forces of evil will dissipate.

A person needs to do subjugation, division, and amelioration due to the Breakage of the Vessels that cast the holy sparks into the "shells." One must separate adverse and foreign thoughts from the Shechinah.[3] This can be done in two ways – one

---

[1] Psalms 144:14
[2] Psalms 92:10
[3] This is the second stage. The first stage is subjugation, in which the foreign thoughts are brought under control. The second stage, separation, entails distinguishing between the false, exterior element of the thought and its inner point of truth – the fallen spark of holiness. The third stage,

general and one particular. The Talmud relates, "How does one dance before the Bride?[1] Beit Shammai said, 'The bride, as she is.' Beit Hillel said, 'A pleasant and gracious bride!'" Beit Shammai felt that in the period of exile, the general way is enough – as she is. Beit Hillel, however, said that we must adorn the bride in a specific way so that she becomes pleasant and gracious.

So too if you are able to purify your thoughts, how good is it to do this specifically through subjugation, division, and amelioration! However, if you cannot, you should at least know in a general way that everything is from G•d. Then you can stand firm and not be pushed from your level by the "shells." You will remain attached to G•d, which is His promise, "And I will give you a path between these standers."[2] This refers to the angels which prevent the external forces and the impure shells from pushing you out of your place.[3]

*Katones Pasim p.27a*

∞

---

amelioration, entails uplifting that truth and incorporating it in the service of G•d.

[1] How does one praise a bride at a wedding?

[2] Zechariah 3:7

[3] A person's place among the angels, who stands before G•d and above the forces of evil, cannot be moved.

10-2 The belief that G•d's glory fills the whole world.

**WHEN** a person knows and believes that G•d's glory fills the whole world and that everything – each and every movement and thought – is from Him, then "all the workers of iniquity will disband."[1] This is the meaning of, "Know the G•d of your fathers."[2]

*Tzafnah Paneach p.86b*

∞

10-3 Prayers of the entire week only ascend on the Sabbath.

"**EVERY** Shabbat, he shall set it up before the L•rd (to be there) continuously; it is an everlasting covenant from the Children of Israel."[3] Each prayer redeems new sparks. However, only on the "Shabbat he shall arrange it" – the prayers of the entire week only ascend on Shabbat during the recitation of Kedusha in the Musaf prayer.

*Katones Pasim p.38b*

---

[1] Psalms 92:10
[2] I Chronicles 28:9
[3] Leviticus 24:8

10-4 Uplifting the sparks and the lowest to the highest level.

"**HOW** does one dance before the bride? Beit Shammai said 'The bride, as she is.' Beit Hillel said, 'A pleasant and gracious bride.'" The Baal Shem Tov explained their disagreement as follows.[1] Beit Shammai said to praise the bride "as she is" by generally knowing that G•d's glory is hidden everywhere. Beit Hillel said to praise the grace and beauty of the bride, for they knew the specific sparks of holiness that had fallen among the shells and how the foreign thoughts come to mind during prayer in order to be repaired. Then, one can separate and remove the shell and raise and adorn the holy spark from among it, making it into a lovely and graceful bride.

*Toldos Yaakov Yosef p. 8d*

∞

---

[1] The Baal Shem Tov interprets this teaching as applying to prayer, which is a manifestation of the *Shechinah*, the spiritual "bride" of the Holy One. Beit Shammai sees prayer as being mixed – good and evil, holy words and distracting thoughts. Thus, he can only praise it "as it is." Beit Hillel knows how to extract the fallen sparks of holiness even within the foreign thought, thereby uplifting that thought and making prayer a beautiful bride for G•d.

# CHAPTER 11

# UNION WITH G•D

11-1 A person's soul and life-force are united with G•d.

**WHAT** is it in a person that feels pleasure or pain? It is his soul, his life-force, for when a person's soul and life-force leave him, he doesn't feel anything. This life-force is united with the Source of all life and creation. When you remember this and think about your source and pray for it, you form a complete unification. This is the meaning of, "Tzaddikim are the messengers of the Matron" – through their own deprivation and suffering, they know and pray for the deficiency of the Shechinah.

*Degel Machane Ephraim, Bechukosai*

∞

11-2 By attaching yourself to the higher worlds during the Amidah you can cleave to the Supernal World even after prayer.

**WHEN** you attach yourself to the higher worlds during the Amidah, you can be raised even higher as our Rabbis have said, "When a person tries to purify himself, they help him."[1] Your

---

[1] Talmud *Shabbat* 104a

thoughts will cling Above, and you will reach the level in which you cleave to the Supernal World even beyond the fixed times of prayer.

*Tzava'as HaRivash 37*

∞

11-3 A person can know if his prayers have been answered if they feel happy after praying.

**A** person can know if his prayers have been answered if he feels happy after he prays. The opposite is true if he feels depressed. Based on this, we can explain the statement, "One day [Rabbi Buna] joined Redemption to Prayer and did not stop smiling the entire day."[1] But surely he joined Redemption to Prayer every day?![2] However, he never knew if his prayers were effective Above. However, on the day that he joined Redemption to Prayer and did not stop smiling, he realized that he had caused Supernal Unification. Thus he was overjoyed.

*Toldos Yaakov Yosef p. 181b*

---

[1] Talmud *Berachos* 9b
[2] The simple meaning of this is that he recited the blessing "Redeemer of Israel" adjacent to the Amidah. However, since the contiguity of these prayers is a normal part of the morning liturgy, the Talmudic commentators have sought alternative ways to understand this statement.

11-4 From efforts to speak with fear and love below, and to cling to the Creator, you get the ability to rise above all.

**SOMETIMES** you are able to attach yourself to Above even when you are not praying. You can do so by thinking you are beyond the dome of the firmament and then strengthen yourself to ascend even higher. Sometimes, even during prayer, you cannot rise up, and you must serve with fear and love below. But from your efforts to speak with fear and love below and to cling to the Creator, you get the ability to rise above the Firmaments, Thrones, Ophanim and Seraphim, and to speak there in that world.[1]

*Tzava'as HaRivash 136*

∞

11-5 When your thoughts cling constantly to G•d, He sends you words to fix yourself and the world.

**WHEN** you become a chariot for wisdom and your thoughts cling constantly to G•d, as it is

---

[1] Referring respectively to *Asiyah, Yetzirah, Beriyah* and *Atzilus.*

written, "to Him you shall cling,"[1] the Holy One sends you words to uplift and sweeten in order to fix yourself and the world.

*Degel Machane Ephraim*

∞

11-6 Whatever you see, remember G•d.

**WHATEVER** you see, remember the Holy One. If it is something you love, remember the love of G•d. If it is something you fear, remember the fear of G•d. Even when you go to the restroom, you should think to yourself, "I am now separating the bad from the good so that the good should remain for the service of G•d." When you go to sleep, think that your mental faculties go to the L•rd and will be strengthened for Divine Service. This is the purpose of yichudim[2].

*Tzava'as HaRivash 22*

∞

---

[1] Deuteronomy 10:20
[2] Unification of supernal elements in (and by) one's mystical devotions in prayer.

11-7 The wicked are an adornment of the Shechinah because they cause the tzaddik to pray from
the narrowness and bring about a union.

**A** bride is bedecked in various garments to
make her desirable for marital union. At the time of
union, however, "they remove their garments in
physical intimacy."[1] It is written, "from my flesh, I
shall behold G•d"[2] – that is, one can discern the
workings of the Supernal from the various aspects
of human life. Prayer is the Shechinah – the
Supernal Bride – and the tzaddik is the bridesmaid.
When he prays from the depths of his heart, he
unites the Bride with the G•d of Israel. This is the
Supernal Union. Therefore, before the union, he
must bedeck the bride with many adornments.
However, he needs to know which garments are the
proper ones, for the tzaddik is like the fruit and the
wicked are like the chaff. As mentioned before, the
wicked serve as a limitation for the tzaddik in order
that they cry out from a state of constriction. Thus,
the wicked are an adornment of the Shechinah,
because they cause the tzaddik to pray and bring
about the union between the Bride and her
Beloved. Then, when the union is made, the

---

[1] Tikunei Zohar 66
[2] Job 19:26.

garments are removed and "all the workers of iniquity will be dispersed."[1]

*Toldos Yaakov Yosef p. 149a*

∞

11-8 When a person remembers that the Divine Presence is in exile, they will feel appalled and a Unification will be made.

**THE** letter aleph is a peleh (wonder).[2] It is clothed in the letter beit, which is two alephs, and the letter gimel, which is three alephs, until the letter tav, which is four hundred alephs.[3] The further a letter is from the beginning of the alphabet, the further it is from vitality, and the more it becomes clothed in the impure shells. But when a person remembers that the Divine Presence is in exile and that a spark of the Shechinah is clothed in these shells, they will feel appalled. Then, "all the workers of iniquity will be dispersed" and a unification will be made. The spark of holiness will

---

[1] Psalms 92:10
[2] In Hebrew, *aleph* and *peleh* consist of the same letters but in differing order, connecting them linguistically and contextually.
[3] The Hebrew letter *tav* has the numerical value of 400.

be removed and reunited with the life-force above, as the verse states, "the living creatures ran and returned."[1] This is its redemption from captivity, and this is the process of "submission." It is as though you are not speaking, only the Divine Presence, whereas "separation" means removing the "shell," and "amelioration" means uplifting it.

*Toldos Yaakov Yosef p. 208d*

∞

---

[1] Ezekiel 1:14

CHAPTER 12

# THE FRUITS
# OF PRAYER

12-1 When you pray, you should concentrate on arousing the letters of Creation.

**WHEN** you pray, you should concentrate on arousing the letters which created the heaven and earth, the upper and lower creatures, and all the worlds. Then, the entire universe will recite the words of prayer with you, for the letters you invoke are the vitality of all creatures. This elevates all things in creation, both in heaven and on earth.

When lofty and spiritual individuals pray with this intention, they also arouse the letters of people on a lower level so that they too can pray with greater concentration and enthusiasm, thus becoming better people.

The Baal Shem Tov told his disciples to pray even for the bird flying overhead. This intention also helps people benefit from the words of Torah with which you admonish them.

*Darchei Tzedek 39*

∞

12-2 Bind yourself to G•d before admonishing the congregation.

**BEFORE** admonishing the congregation, you must bind yourself to G•d. Then you can attach and bind yourself to the congregation in unity and oneness, for both the leaders of the generation and the people share the same root. Then G•d will be with you, and you will all ascend together and unite with Him. Thus it is said, "Fortunate is one who takes sinners by the hand to uplift them."[1] Then, there is an immediate effect when you admonish the congregation. This also applies to raising them up by means of prayer.

*Toldos Yaakov Yosef p.66c*

∞

12-3 Your prayer will bear fruit and offspring both in this and in the higher worlds.

"**THERE** shall not be barren a man or woman among you or among your cattle."[2] Rabbi Chanina ben Levi said: "The Holy One said, 'Your prayers

---

[1] Zohar 2:128b
[2] Deuteronomy 7:14

will not be barren; rather, they will ascend and bear fruit.'"1

Sometimes you pray for one thing, yet receive another. At other times, your prayers bear fruit only in the upper worlds. This, then, is the meaning of, "there shall not be man or woman barren among you or among your cattle" – letters of prayer will not be barren; rather, they will bear fruit and offspring. There is yet a further guarantee. The verse continues, "or among your cattle" – even your low, mundane requests will bear fruit. Thus, your prayers will achieve everything, bearing fruit and offspring, so that even your cattle – the literal request in the words such as livelihood and health – will result from your prayers.

*Degel Machane Ephraim, Eikev*

∞

12-4 As soon as you pray, you should also believe that your words are answered.

**THE** essence of prayer in exile is faith, which means believing that G•d's glory fills the entire world. This raises the "feet" of the Shechinah. You

---

1 Midrash Rabbah Devorim 3:6

should also believe that as soon as you pray, your words are answered. Though you sometimes do not get what you requested, that is only because it is concealed from you.[1] Perhaps, your request was fulfilled on a universal level, and even though you made an individual request, your suffering may be for your own good. By asking for yourself, you make your prayers material when they should be purely spiritual. Thus, they became a barrier.

*Ben Poras Yosef p. 127a*

∞

12-5 Knowing if your service of G•d is absolutely true and selfless.

**THE** way to know if your service of G•d is absolutely true and selfless is whether you remain humble after you pray with great concentration and do not consider yourself deserving of reward.

*Ohr HaGanuz LaTzaddikim, Ki Seitzei*

∞

---

[1] The manner of its fulfillment is concealed from you.

12-6 With every prayer and word of Torah uttered with concentration, you unite the World of Speech with the World of Thought.

**THREE** books are opened on Rosh Hashanah – the Book of the Completely Wicked, the Book of the Completely Righteous, and the Book of the Intermediaries. The righteous are immediately written and sealed for life; the wicked are immediately written and sealed for death; and the intermediaries are left hanging until Yom Kippur. If they are worthy, they are written for life; if not, they are written for death."[1]

The above-mentioned books refer to words. All the holy words of the completely righteous – their prayers and Torah study – unite speech within the realm of thought. For you must believe that with every prayer and word of Torah uttered with concentration, you certainly unite the realm of speech with the realm of thought. Even when you pray and your requests are not granted, nevertheless the efforts that unite speech and thought cause the same union Above. Those individuals whose sole intention is to unite these two worlds are perfect tzaddikim.

---

[1] Talmud Rosh Hashanah 16b

Our Rabbis said, "One may not pray except with a koved rosh"[1] – with the realization that whatever you lack personally is also lacking Above. We are also taught, "Even if the king greets you, do not stop (praying)."[2] When a person prays with concentration, G•d takes pride in the realm of speech. This pride spreads though all the worlds even to the one who is praying.[3] Thus, be careful not to break your connection with G•d and not to become proud of praying with such concentration.

"Intermediaries" pray that G•d should also fulfill their mundane requests. They are left waiting until Yom Kippur. They must tarry until the thoughts and intentions of their heart are revealed. If their intentions were for G•d's sake when they made their request, they are also written in the Book of the Intermediaries for life for these intentions unite speech and thought.

*Tzava'as HaRivash 123*

∞

---

[1] Literally, a heavy head. Referring to an attitude of reverence. Mishna *Berachos* 5:1
[2] Talmud *Berachos* 30b
[3] The feeling of pride a person can feel during prayer is a fallen manifestation of the pride that G•d Himself takes in the prayers.

# CHAPTER 13

# BACK IN THE WORLD

## 13-1 Attaching thoughts and words to G•d.

**WHEN** I attach my thoughts to G•d, I let my mouth speak whatever it wants. I bind the words to their source in G•d for everything has a root in the sefirot above. At times, I sit among people who are discussing mundane things and attach myself to G•d so that I bind all of their words Above.

*Likkutim Yekarim p. 3c*

∞

## 13-2 The goal of a tzaddik is to always be attached to G•d.

**"THE** everyday speech of Torah scholars deserves study."[1] The highest goal of a tzaddik is to be attached to G•d without a moment's break. Even when he speaks about mundane things, he must not break his deveikut. The same applies to performing a commandment because thinking about doing the mitzvah can also break one's devotion. A person must be very wary of this. Our Rabbis said that one must learn to speak about mundane things that are necessary so as not to lose one's focus.

*Divrei Moshe*

---

[1] Talmud *Sukkah* 21b

∞

13-3 King David's only desire was to constantly unify G•d and the Shechinah.

"**I** will walk at ease, for I have sought Your precepts."[1] King David praised himself for being able to walk in the markets and streets "for I have sought Your precepts" – he never wanted anything but Supernal Unification. His only desire was to constantly unify G•d and the Shechinah.

*Degel Machane Ephraim, Ki Seitzei*

∞

13-4 Serve G•d while telling stories or speaking about mundane things.

**I** heard and saw how my grandfather (the Baal Shem Tov) would tell stories or speak about mundane things, yet all the while, he served G•d with his pure, clear wisdom.

*Degel Machane Ephraim, Vayeishev*

---

[1] Psalms 119:45

**13-5 There are Supernal Unifications in every word or story.**

**THERE** are Supernal unifications in every word and mundane story. I heard from the Baal Shem Tov that he would unite himself Above with his everyday tales.

*Toldos Yaakov Yosef p. 41b*

∞

**13-6 Words of Torah spoken with fear of G•d makes its mark.**

**EACH** word of Torah or wisdom spoken with fear of G•d makes its mark. The everyday speech of some Torah scholars also makes its mark, and thus, they do great things for G•d.

*Degel Machane Ephraim, Chayeh Sarah*

∞

**13-7 G•d wants us to serve Him in all ways.**

**YOU** must serve G•d with all of your might for everything is needed and G•d wants us to serve

Him in all situations. This means that sometimes a person talks with others and is therefore unable to study, but they still must remain attached to G•d. Likewise, when a person is on the road and is unable to pray or study Torah as usual, they must serve G•d in different ways. But they shouldn't get upset for G•d wants them to serve Him in all ways – sometimes like this and sometimes like that. Thus, He arranges for the need for a person to travel or to talk with others in order to serve Him in this and other ways.

*Tzava'as HaRivash 2-3*

∞

13-8 G•d is always putting you into situations for your own good.

**WISE** people know how to perform yichudim even when they are conversing with their friends, as is taught, "A woman's voice is alluring."[1] To remove depression, open some business or become involved in some activity and cause a yichud with this vessel. Likewise, when you see something wrong in another person or if he disturbs your learning and

---

[1] Talmud *Berachos* 24a

prayer, remember that G•d is doing it to you for your own good.

*Toldos Yaakov Yosef, Vayeitzei*

∞

13-9 The most useful words are sent to one whose thoughts constantly cling to G•d,

**WHEN** you begin to study or simply discuss day-to-day matters, pay attention to what you are saying, whether it is on the topic love, fear, compassion, competitiveness, praise, relationships or some form of control.[1] Then bind yourself to that attribute.

*Likkutim Yekarim p. 4b*

∞

13-10 Bind yourself to whatever attribute you are thinking.

**EVEN** when you speak to a friend in the street, do so with fear and love for speech is

---

[1] Each attribute being related to a particular sefirah.

composed of letters, as the Talmud states, "They see her speaking with one in the market."[1] Your speech should always be with the One and Only.

*Ohr HaGanuz LaTzaddikim, Pekudei*

∞

13-11 Speech should always be with fear and love.

**IN** all your ways know Him."[2] Even when you simply relate events to your friends, you should intend to draw close to G•d. Then, if someone asks you to do some mitzvah or good deed, you can fulfill their request since you're already close to G•d. This is the essence of the letter vav, which bends down to the letter hey to uplift it.[3]

*Toldos Yaakov Yosef, Terumah*

∞

---

[1] Talmud *Kesuvos* 13a
[2] Proverbs 3:6
[3] The last two letters of the Tetragrammaton are *vav* and *hey*, which signify Divine effluence sustaining the universe.

**13-12 Your intent should always to be draw close to G•d.**

**AFTER** you pray, you must be careful not to become angry or exhibit some other improper behavior, G•d forbid. If you pray with fear, you may become angry.[1] If you pray with love, you can sometimes feel an inappropriate kind of love. This applies to every character trait. The solution, then, is to study Torah or do some act of work immediately after prayer, as we are taught, "All Torah that is not accompanied by work will ultimately be nullified and lead to sin."[2]

*Degel Machane Ephraim, Ki Sisa*

∞

**13-13 Thought is a complete entity.**

**WHEN** you think about bad things, you reduce your mind to the level of those things and cut yourself off from the Infinite. Then strict judgments can rest upon you. So too when you think about

---

[1] Anger is a lower manifestation of awe and fear of G•d. Every emotion and character trait has both an elevated form, which is manifested in moments of spiritual awakening, and a debased form that surfaces in times of distance from G•d.
[2] Mishna *Avos* 2:2

material things, your thoughts become reduced to that place and you draw yourself there, for thought is a complete entity.

*Kesser Shem Tov, part 2, p. 2*

∞

# GLOSSARY

**Achiyah HaShiloni:** The Heavenly teacher of the Baal Shem Tov. In prior incarnations, Achiyah HaShaloni witnessed the exodus from Egypt, was a prophet during the time of King David, and taught Elijah the Prophet.

**Amidah:** (lit. standing); It is a prayer that is to be recited inaudible in a standing position; also referred to as the Shemonah Esreh (eighteen benedictions), the main section of daily prayer.

**Arizal:** acronym for Eloki Rabbi Yitzchak — the Divinely inspired Rabbi Yitzcahk Luria (1535 — 1572) — whose teachings became central for virtually all Kabbalistic thought thereafter.

**Asiyah:** (lit. deed); The final level in the Divine creative process which includes the physical universe.

**Atzilus:** (lit. emanation); The realm of spiritual existence which, although encompassing attributes which have a specific definition, is in a state of infinity and at one with the Infinite Divine Light.

**Beriyah:** (lit. creation); The realm of spiritual existence which represents the first beginnings of a consciousness of self.

**Binah:** (lit. comprehension); The stage of the intellectual process that develops abstract conception, giving it breadth and depth.

**Barchu:** (lit. bless); One of the responsive readings in congregational prayer.

**Breaking of the Vessels:** In the primordial Shattering of the Vessels, 288 sparks of holiness fell into the lower worlds.

**Bittul ha-yesh**: The annihilation of somethingness.

**Chassid:** (lit. pious one); One who observes beyond the letter of the law; A follower of the Chassidic movement (pl. chassidim).

**Chayot**: Angels from the world of Yitzirah.

**Chazan:** (lit. cantor); One who leads the congregation in prayer.

**Cheder:** (lit. room); A Torah school for young children.

**Chesed:** (lit. kindness); The Divine attribute of benevolence.

**Chochmah:** (lit. wisdom); The stage of the intellectual process for abstract conception.

**Daat:** (lit. knowledge); The third stage of the intellectual process at which concepts, having proceeded from seminal intuition through meditative gestation, now mature into their corresponding dispositions or attributes of character.

**Dinim:** Divine judgments.

**Dveikut:** (lit. clinging); A profound concentration and spiritual attachment.

**Gadlut:** (lit. greatness); The expanded state of consciousness and existence.

**Gevurah:** (lit. might); The attribute of restraint, associated with the restriction of Divine emanation.

**Hod:** (lit. splendor); One of the Divine attributes.

**Kabbalah:** (lit. received tradition); The body of Jewish mystical teachings.

**Katnut:** (lit. smallness); The constricted and narrow state of consciousness and existence.

**Kavanah:** Intention.

**Kedusha:** (lit. holiness); A passage in the public prayer service with portions recited responsively by the chazan and congregation.

**Kelipot:** (lit. shells); The outer coverings which conceal Divinity within all creation; hence, the unholy side of the universe.

**Koved Rosh:** (lit. a heavy head}; Referring to an attitude of reverence.

**Kriyat Shema:** The recitation of the daily declaration of faith, recited in the morning and evening prayers, as well as before retiring to sleep.

**Machzor:** The prayer book used specifically for the High Holidays.

**Malchut:** (lit. kingship); The Divine attribute of might or power.

**Midot:** Divine and mortal attributes of character, spiritual emotions, and mental states.

**Minyan:** (lit. number); The quorum of ten men necessary for communal prayer.

**Mitzvah:** (lit. commandment); One of the 613 commandments found in the Torah; a generally good deed

**Mochin:** (lit. brains); The three attributes or stages of the intellectual process.

**Moshiach:** (lit. the anointed one); The Messiah.

**Nefesh:** soul: in Kabbalistic doctrine, the fifth and lowest level of the soul that vitalizes the body.

**Ne'ilah:** (lit. closing); The fifth and final prayer service recited on Yom Kippur.

**Netzach:** (lit. victory); The Divine attribute of eternity.

**Ophanim**: Angel from world of Asiyah.

**Penimiyut:** (lit. innerness); The endeavor to make one's deeds and attainments an integral part of one's being; the opposite of superficiality.

**Pesukei D'Zimrah:** (lit. verses of praise); The selection of passages which appear early in the morning prayer service and lead into the declaration of faith.

**Ramban:** Rabbi Moshe ben Nachman, also known as Nachmanides (1194-1270).

**Rosh Hashanah:** (lit. head of the year); The solemn New Year holiday.

**Satan:** The Accusing Angel.

**Sefirah:** One of the Divine attributes or emanations which are the source of the corresponding faculties of the soul.

**Seraphim:** Fiery Angels from world of Briyah.

**Shabbat:** (lit. rest); The Sabbath, the Divinely-ordained day of rest on the seventh day of the week.

**Shamash:** (lit. attendant); The synagogue beadle.

**Shechinah:** The Divine Presence; sometimes identified as the sephirah of Malkut or Knesset Israel. The collectivity of Jewish souls

**Shefah:** The flow of Divine life-force into creation.

**Shema:** The daily declaration of faith recited in the morning and evening prayers, as well as before retiring to sleep.

**Shochet:** (lit. ritual slaughterer); One who slaughters and inspects cattle and fowl in the ritually prescribed manner for kosher consumption.

**Tiferet:** (lit. beauty); The Divine attribute of compassion.

**Tzaddik:** A wholly righteous person (pl. tzaddikim).

**Yesod:** (lit. foundation); One of the Divine attributes.

**Yetzirah:** (lit. formation); The realm of spiritual existence in which the limited nature of the created beings takes on form and definition.

**Yichudim:** Unification of supernal elements in and by one's mystical devotions in prayer.

**Yom Kippur:** The Day of Atonement.

**Zeir Anpin:** (lit. "small countenance,) The collection of Divine attributes excluding Malchut (might).

# BIBLIOGRAPHY - HEBREW

Ateret Tiferet Yisrael, Rabbi Yisrael of Behofaleh, Warsaw 5631 (1871)

Avodat Yisrael, Rabbi Yisrael, Koznitzer Magid, New York 5732 (1972)

Beit Yisrael, Rabbi Tzvj Hirsch of Ziditchov, Lemberg 5594 (1834)

Be'er Mayan Chaim, Rabbi Chaim of Ohalov, Warsaw 5636 (1876)

Birkat Avraham, Rabbi Avraham David of Butchach, Warsaw 5575 (1815)

Butzna DeNehorah, Rabbi Baruch of Mezibush, Lemberg 5640 (1880)

Degel Machaneh Ephraim, Rabbi Moshe Chaim Ephraim of Sudylkov, New York 5707 (1947)

Dibras Shlomo, Rabbi Shlomo of Lutzk, Zalkiev 5608 (1848)

Divrei Moshe, Rabbi Moshe of Dlina, Zalkiev 5625 (1865)

---

Dudajrn BaSadeh, Rabbi Reuven Horwitz of Zarnavitza, Lemberg 5619 (1859).

Etz HaDaat Tov, Rabbi Uziel Meisels, Warsaw, 5623 (1863).

Geulat Yisrael, Rabbi Yehoshua Avraham of Zhitimar, Lemberg, 5610 (1850).

Ginzei Yosef, Rabbi Yosef Blach of Satanov, Lemberg, 5552 (1792).

Hanhagot Yesharot, collected from the works of Rabbi Yaakov Yosef of Polonoye, Lashtzov, 5576 (1816).

Imrei Tzadikim, the teachings of the Baal Shem Tov and Mezricher Magid, compiled by Rabbi Chaim Krasna, Husatin, 5559 (1799).

Kesonet Pasirn, Rabbi Yaakov Yosef of Polonoye, Lemberg, 5626 (1866).

Kitvei Kodesh, collected teachings of the Baal Shem Tov and his disciples, Warsaw, 5645 (1885).

Kochavey Or, the teachings of Rabbi Nachman, compiled by Rabbi Shmuel Horowitz, Jerusalem, 5721 (1951).

Likutei Amarim (see Magid Devarav LeYaakov).

Likutei Amarim (see Tanya).

Likutei Moharan, the teachings of Rabbi Nachman, compiled by Rabbi Nathan of Nemerov.

Magid Devarav LeYaakov teachings of the Mezricher Magid, compiled by Rabbi Shiomo of Lutsk, Jerusalem, 5731 (1971).

Meor VeShemesh Rabbi Kelonemos Kalmon of Krackow; in Chumash Mikrot Gedolot.

Midrash Pinchas, Rabbi Pinchas of Koretz, Jerusalem, 5731 (1971).

Nevei Tzadikim, in Shoshanah LeDavid.

Noam Elimelech, Rabbi Elimelech of Lizensk, Jerusalem.

Notzer Chesed, Rabbi Yitzchok Isaac of Kamarna, Lemberg 5616 (1856).

Ohev Yisrael, Rabbi Avraham Yehoshua Heschel of Opt, Jerusalem 5725 (1965).

Or HaErnet (see Imrei Tzadikim).

Or Torah, teachings of the Baal Shem Tov and Mezricher Magid, Lemberg 5622 (1862).

Orach LeChaim, Rabbi Avraham Chaim of Zlatchov, Zalkiev 5577 (1817).

Otzar HaChaim, Rabbi Yitzchak Isaac of Kamarna, Lemberg 5618 (1858).

Pri Chairn, Rabbi Avraham Chaim of Zlachav.

Pri HaAretz, Rabbi Menechem Mendel of Vitebsk, Jerusalem 5729 (1969).

Rabbi Yibi, Rabbi Yaakov Yosef of Ostrog, New York, 5714 (1954).

Rishfei Esh, Rabbi Mordecai of Neshchez, printed with Rabbi Yibi.

Sefer Baal Shem Tov, compiled by Rabbi Shimon Mendel of Givartchav, Jerusalem, 5722 (1962).

Shivchei HaBaal Shem Tov, compiled by Rabbi Dov Baer of Linitz, Jerusalem 5729 (1969).

Shivchei HaRan, life and teachings of Rabbi Nachman, compiled by Rabbi Nathan of Nemerov, Jerusalem, 5721 (1961). Available in English, as Rabbi Nachman's Wisdom, New York, 1973.

Sichot HaRan, teachings of Rabbi Nachman, compiled by Rabbi Nathan of Nemerov, Jerusalem, 5721 (1961). Available in English, see preceding.

Sichot Moharan, teachings of Rabbi Nachman, compiled by Rabbi Nathan of Nemerov, printed with Chayah Moharan, Jerusalem, 5722 (1962).

Tanya (Likutei Amarim), Rabbi Schneur Zalman of Liadi, New York, 5723 (1963). Available in English, Kehot, New York, 1969.

Tiferet Beth Levi, Rabbi Shlomo Gutman of Jasse, Jasse, 5770 (1910).

Toledot Aaron, Rabbi Aaron of Zhitamar, Berdichov, 5577 (1817).

Torat HaMagid, teachings of the Mezricher Magid, compiled by Rabbi Yisrael Klapholtz, Tel Aviv, 5729 (1969).

T'shvat Chen, Rabbi Gedaliah of Linitz, Lemberg, 5622 (1862).

Turei Zahav, Rabbi Benyamin of Zlazitz, Mohelov, 5576 (1816).

Tzafenat Pa'aneach, Rabbi Yaakov Yosef of Polonoye, Koretz 5542 (1782).

Tzetel Katan, Rabbi Elimelch of Lizensk, printed with Noam Elimelech, q.v. VaY'Chal Moshe, Rabbi Moshe Elyakim Brieh, Lemberg, 5628 (1868).

Yemei Moharnat, diary of Rabbi Nathan of Nemerov, disciple of Rabbi Nachman, New York, 5730 (1970).

Zichron Zot, Rabbi Yaakov Yitzchok, the Seer of Lublin, Israel 5733 (1973).

Zohar Chai, Rabbi Yitzchok Isaac of Kamarna, Tel Aviv, 5731 (1971).

# BIBLIOGRAPHY - ENGLISH

1. THE PATH OF THE BAAL SHEM TOV
   by Rabbi David Sears
2. ESSENTIAL PAPERS ON CHASSIDISM
   Edited by Gershon David Hundert
3. THE LIGHT BEYOND
   by Rabbi Aryeh Kaplan
4. TZAVA'AT HARIVASH
   by Rabbi Jacob Immanuel Schochet
5. THE LIGHT AND FIRE OF THE BAAL SHEM TOV
   by Maggid Yitzhak Buxbaum
6. THE BESHT
   by Professor Emanuel Etkes
7. CHASSIDIC MASTERS
   by Rabbi Aryeh Kaplan
8. The Religious Thought of Chassidim
   by Rabbi Norman Lamm
9. HASSIDIC PRAYER
   by Louis Jacobs
10. YOUR WORD IS FIRE
    by Arthur Green and Barry Holtz
11. HASIDISM AS MYSTICISM
    by Rivka Schatz Uffenheimer

# WWW.MEZUZAH.NET

## Home of the World Wide
## Mezuzah Campaign

The fundamental goal of The World Wide Mezuzah Campaign is to unify the Jewish people. By fulfilling the mitzvah of Mezuzah, this unity can be accomplished by each Jewish person: man, woman or child. The mitzvah can be easily fulfilled by affixing a Mezuzah on the "Doorpost of Your House or upon Your Gates," as required by Jewish law.

Purchase Mezuzahs written in Israel by a Certified Scribe, then checked by a computer for accuracy and finally checked by a second Certified Scribe before we send it to you. Our Mezuzahs are of a very high quality, and they are beautifully written. They are shipped to you in a Mezuzah case ready to mount on your door.

www.mezuzah.net
The World Wide Mezuzah Campaign.
A project of the Baal Shem Tov Foundation
a 501(c)(3), non-profit organization

# Baal Shem Tov Times

Spreading the light of the legendary
Kabbalah Master and Mystic

# Rabbi Yisrael Baal Shem Tov

## -A weekly email publication-

**Regular Features:**

Baal Shem Tov Story
Torah Baal Shem Tov
Heart of Prayer
Divine Light
Kesser Shem Tov

Subscribe to receive your FREE weekly
e-mail edition at
www.baalshemtov.com

# ABOUT THE AUTHOR

**TZVI MEIR COHN** (Howard M. Cohn) attended Yeshiva Hadar Hatorah in Crown Heights, Brooklyn after completing his university studies in Engineering and Law. While studying at the Yeshiva, he discovered a deep connection to the stories and teachings of the Baal Shem Tov. Later, he founded the Baal Shem Tov Foundation which is dedicated to spreading the teachings of the Baal Shem Tov in order to hasten the final redemption of the Jewish people. To spread the teachings of the Baal Shem Tov, Tzvi Meir created a website BaalShemTov.com and publishes a weekly newsletter, the Baal Shem Tov Times. Tzvi Meir gives live presentations of his original music and Baal Shem Tov stories to welcoming audiences. Presently, Tzvi Meir practices as a Patent and Trademark Attorney (www.CohnPatents.com) in Cleveland, Ohio.

# ALSO BY BST PUBLISHING

BAAL SHEM TOV FAITH LOVE AND JOY Vol. I

BAAL SHEM TOV DIVINE LIGHT Vol. II

BAAL SHEM TOV HEART OF PRAYER Vol. III

BAAL SHEM TOV GENESIS Vol. I

BAAL SHEM TOV EXODUS Vol. II

BAAL SHEM TOV LEVITICUS Vol. III

BAAL SHEM TOV NUMBERS Vol. IV

BAAL SHEM TOV DEUTERONOMY Vol. V

BAAL SHEM TOV HOLY DAYS Vol. VI

www.ingramcontent.com/pod-product-compliance
Lightning Source LLC
LaVergne TN
LVHW011227080426
835509LV00005B/365